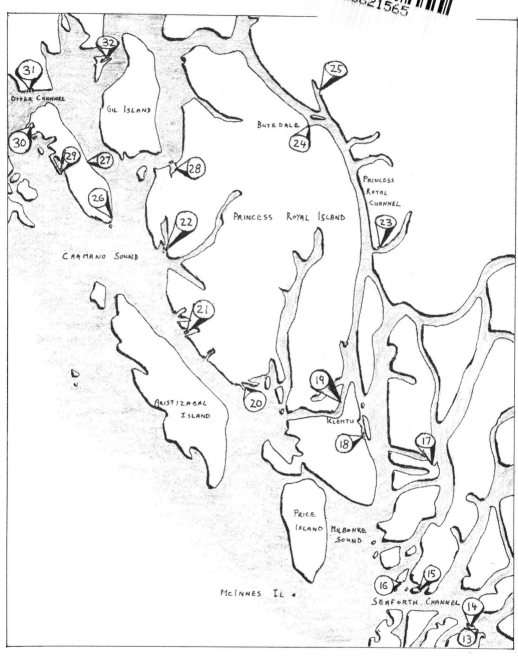

Otter Channel

Gil Island

Butedale

Princess Royal Channel

Princess Royal Island

Caamano Sound

Aristizabal Island

Klemtu

Price Island

Milbanke Sound

McInnes Il.

Seaforth Channel

Far-Away Places

Far-Away Places

50 Places

Anchorages on the Northwest Coast

Iain Lawrence

ORCA BOOK PUBLISHERS

Canadian Cataloguing in Publication Data
Lawrence, Iain, 1955–
  Far-away places

  Includes index.
  ISBN 1-55143-033-9

  1. Boats and boating—British Columbia—Queen Charlotte Sound Region—Guidebooks. 2. Boats and boating—British Columbia—Hecate Strait Region—Guidebooks. 3. Queen Charlotte Sound Region (B.C.)—Guidebooks. 4. Hecate Strait Region (B.C.)—Guidebooks. I. Title.
GV776.15.B7L38 1995   917.11'1044   C95-910217-5

Reproduction of information from Canadian Hydrographic Service *Sailing Directions* in this publication are for illustrative purposes only, they do not meet the requirements of the Charts and Publication Regulations and are not to be used for navigation. The appropriate *Sailing Directions*, corrected up-to-date, and the relevant Canadian Hydrographic Service charts required under the Charts and Publications Regulations of the Canada Shipping Act must be used for navigation.

Contact the Canadian Hydrographic Service to obtain information on local dealers and available charts and publications or to order charts and publications directly:

Chart Sales and Distribution Office
Canadian Hydrographic Service
Department of Fisheries and Oceans
Institute of Ocean Sciences, Patricia Bay
9860 West Saanich Road
Sidney, BC V8L 4B2
telephone: 604-363-6358 fax: 604-363-6841

Cover design by Christine Toller
Front cover photograph by Mark Hobson
Back cover photographs by Iain Lawrence
Interior photographs and maps by Iain Lawrence
Interior illustrations by Donald Lawrence

Printed and bound in Canada

Orca Book Publishers
PO Box 5626, Station B
Victoria, BC Canada
V8R 6S4

Orca Book Publishers
PO Box 468
Custer, WA USA
98240-0468

10 9 8 7 6 5 4 3 2 1

*For my parents, who began sailing together
in their seventies, with all my love and admiration*

≈ ACKNOWLEDGEMENTS ≈

Many people contributed to this book, most without even knowing it. So thanks go first of all to everyone I've met in harbours big and small who answered my ever-asked questions: "What's your favourite place on the coast?" and "Could you show me that on the chart?"

But above all, two people deserve special thanks. Kristin Miller has been a part of my life for nearly a decade, and together we've travelled some five thousand sea miles to places near and far. She has given me encouragement and help, inspiration and enjoyment. My brother Donald did the drawings for this book and critiqued the manuscript as we sat at anchor in many of the harbours listed here. He shared his expertise on sea kayaking and beach camping, and shared his berth with the dog.

And, finally, I'd like to thank the Little People of Harwood Bay and the captains and crew of these wonderful boats: *Bluefin, Aurora, Rupert Pelican, Grizzly Bear, Kumquat, Wind Speed, Far Reach, Luigi,* and *Yaba.* The coast is a better place, a little less desolate, because you are there.

≈ CONTENTS ≈

≈ INTRODUCTION ≈

Most boaters travelling north on the Inside Passage stick to the regular route like cars on a highway. They pass Cape Caution and Egg Island, stick to the freeway through Bella Bella, Boat Bluff and Butedale. At night they pull off into the same places, like campers to KOA parks, and when they get to where they're going, they turn around and take the same route back.

Well, there's nothing wrong with that. It's a wonderful trip, and the Inside Passage certainly gets you where you're going, if all you want to do is go. The fishboats use it for that, the ferries and the cruise ships, and pleasure boats by the hundreds. It's a rare moment in the summer not to have another boat in sight anywhere along the 240 miles from Cape Calvert to Prince Rupert. After all, that's why they call it a marine highway.

Some people find the traffic comforting. They anchor in the middle of huge jams of boats, squeezing in like musk oxen. They set up chairs high on the flying bridge and watch every movement, every coming and going, through binoculars that they're forever polishing, like reading glasses. And they never, never—well, hardly ever—go ashore.

But this book is not for them.

Others find the traffic crowding. And these people take the exits that all highways have, and find their own routes along the sidestreets and backroads of the coast. They put away the marine atlas with its ruler-straight red lines, and pull out the charts—the real charts—with big compass roses and land that looks like land.

And they go exploring.

They find lonely beaches and quiet anchorages. They watch whales and porpoises in the daytime, and listen at night to the howls of wolves instead of the rattle of generators. They can't find an unspoiled coast; there isn't one any more. But they really can go days at a time without meeting another boat. And they can go out on deck when the sun's long down, and see nothing but darkness in every direction, where the only lights are those of the stars.

It is for these people, whether they travel in tiny kayaks or huge luxury yachts, that I hope this book will be a bit of a guide, a bit of an inspiration. These are places we have found over several years of poking along the backstreets. They are places where the kayaker can often find a comfortable beach for the night, where the boater can drop an anchor and happily stay a day or two, or longer. They are some of our favourite places.

≈ FOR THE LITTLE PEOPLE ≈

Our boat is just twenty-seven feet long. There's not enough height in the cabin to stand up, not enough room in the cockpit to lie down. But *Nid* is enormous compared to some of the boats that travel the north coast, the kayaks and skiffs of the Little People.

It was Kristin who named them that. She meant it in a kindly way and it seemed to fit them well. The Little People are elusive. We saw their campsites and their firepits years before we saw the first one on the water. They're hardy and brave, and they can fit themselves into places we could never hope to reach.

I envy the Little People for their freedom and admire them for their endurance. They see a lot more than most boaters and, consequently, their stories are far more interesting.

As far as possible I've tried to make this book useful to the people who go down to the sea in very small boats. I've included notes on good beaches and mentioned streams where water can be easily collected. Where we've found established campsites, I've recorded that as well.

My brother is a kayaker. In the summer of 1994, while I was compiling final notes and collecting photographs for this book, my brother joined me for a three-week voyage out of Bella Bella. He brought one of his three kayaks, a big Klepper that folded— as only a German boat could—into a pair of canvas duffle bags. He's paddled with it down the east coast of Maine and the west coast of Scotland, but this was his first trip to the north coast. And it gave me a small introduction to the lives of the Little People.

On a cold evening, in a firehose of rain, we towed his *Ziploc Schooner* into a bay just north of Superstition Point. There were three kayakers on the beach, huddled under tarps and canvas shelters, the smoke from their fire clinging to the trees. We'd caught a salmon off the reef, and once we'd anchored, I started cutting it into thick steaks.

"Maybe we should give some to the Little People," I said.

"That would be nice," said Donald. But neither of us wanted to put on raingear again, to bail the dinghy and to row to shore. And we quickly convinced ourselves that they wouldn't need our salmon. Surely they would have caught their own—the fish were jumping like fleas. And it wasn't a very big salmon at any rate. They would likely have felt insulted merely by the offer.

So I put the steaks in the frying pan, in a bath of soy sauce and brown sugar. And as they sizzled away, I kept looking out at the Little People. They were all three in raingear, shuttling back and forth from their fire to the tarps.

"I feel sorry for those guys," I said.

Donald looked up from the settee. He was reading as the rain hammered on the deck above him. "Why?" he said, surprised.

"Well, look at them." I pointed with the spatula. "Sitting down to their mean little dinner. Huddled under their crude shelters." I meant it to sound rather sad, but Donald only laughed.

"Yes," he said. "It's a very Dickensian way to travel."

In the hierarchy of boats cruising up and down the coast,

we're right in there next to the Little People. We spend as much time on shore as we can; we often cook on the beach, and always shower there. We get our drinking water from the small streams that dry to trickles in the heat spells of mid-summer.

We've even learned the kayakers' trick for lying on a beach: aim yourself downhill instead of across the slope, and the sand fleas hop right past you. And sometimes we talk of going on a long trip in a small boat, if we can ever pry ourselves loose from all our comforts.

≈ GETTING OFF THE HIGHWAY ≈

There are two major routes through the sheltered channels of the north coast. The heavily travelled Inside Passage hugs the mainland shore as much as possible. At Butedale, its furthest inland point, the passage is more than thirty-five miles from the open waters of Hecate Strait. It's the well-beaten path of the Alaska cruising guides, the quickest and simplest way to hurry through the north coast.

The second route follows the wider passages of Laredo Channel, Estevan Sound and Principe Channel. It's never more than ten miles from the open water and, in places, lies fully exposed to winds and swell coming in from the Strait. Wider passages and a straight-line course from southeast to northwest open the route to prevailing winds. But what the small-boat navigator loses in shelter, he gains in scenery, solitude, and the chance for exploration.

For the sailor this "other inside passage" is a true windfall. He finds a steady breeze—or more—and lots of sea room. We've sailed non-stop for forty hours at a time, in a warm and steady breeze, without coming closer than half a mile to another boat. There's a fraction of the traffic here that one encounters in Grenville Channel. And this is a strong attraction also for the Little People—the kayakers and rowers and dinghy sailors—who will find a greater choice of beaches and haul-out spots than the Inside Passage has to offer.

Because the summer winds are predominantly from the northwest, it's easier to travel south than north down the outer channel. And since Kristin and I live in Prince Rupert—and end up hurrying home in the last days of August—we usually take one part or another of the Inside Passage to avoid headwinds in the outer route. Our boat's an old gaff-rigged cutter; *Nid's* a delight to sail on a reach, but a curse to windward.

In five places the routes cross and converge. The small-boat navigator can weave back and forth from one passage to the other without ever backtracking. And if he even once ventures west to the outer channels, he'll go home with a far better picture of the north coast than he will if he sticks to the Inside Passage going both north and south. There's no proper path to take; the navigator will choose his own way among the myriad of islands along the way. He'll base his decisions on weather conditions and his own personal preferences.

For this reason I've arranged the anchorages in this book, not according to established routes, but in four blocks from south to north. The best way to use the maps is not as a route planner, but as a list of possible stops, wherever your voyage takes you. Go exploring; go a'roving. In the words of American novelist Sarah Jewett, "A harbour, even if it is a little harbour, is a good thing."

DIVIDING POINTS

Hakai Passage

The usual route north, the Inside Passage, crosses the eastern end of Hakai Passage and continues up Fitz Hugh Sound to Lama Passage. Even those who make the sidetrip to Pruth Bay will often exit through the north end of Kwakshua Channel only to cut back again to Fitz Hugh Sound. But since the creation of Hakai Recreation Area, more boats are finding an alternative route through the small islands surrounding Kildidt Sound, a route that takes them to the heart of this magnificent park. It's a huge thing, 123,000 hectares, stretching nearly the full length of Calvert Island's west coast, north to the Goose Islands and the entrance to Hunter Channel.

From the top of Kwakshua Channel you can find a sheltered route to the area by crossing Hakai to the narrow passages of Ward Channel and Nalau Passage. A more open route leads west of the Pointers and north through either Kildidt Sound or Queens Sound. Watch for the tide; it can run through Hakai Passage at four knots, and the flood will set you quickly toward the North Pointers.

The outside route offers a choice of continuing north by ei-

ther Hunter Channel or Raymond Passage to rejoin the Inside Passage. Both are open to Queens Sound and require caution in dealing with strong tidal currents. Read the cautions in the *Sailing Directions* before entering Queens Sound.

Southbound boats can also use these outside routes and then enter Hakai Pass from the west. The south-going ebb tides are very strong through the islands at the northern end of Queens Sound, an advantage only until they're met by opposing winds. Good pilotage is called for, as well as the time to wait for favourable conditions.

By any route or either direction, fog can be a concern in the Hakai area. It blows in from the sea in great, thick banks at any time of the day.

On the Inside Passage, nine miles from Hakai, is the cannery village of Namu. Once a thriving part of the fishing industry, and more lately a popular stopping place for cruisers, it is now somewhere in between the two, and rapidly becoming neither.

Commercial fishboats were crossing Queen Charlotte Sound and coming all the way to Namu just for ice the first time we stopped there in 1989. The docks were crowded, the liquor store was almost sold out, and there were vast, empty shelves in the store. We walked from one end of the boardwalk to the other, hiked to the lake and back, took long showers at the free stalls. And we sat on a bench outside the cafe and waited for it to open. Oddly, it was closed for lunch. Namu was that kind of place; we liked it a lot.

B.C. Packers didn't cater to pleasure boats, but it made them welcome. Though they were encouraged to use the outer floats exposed to harbour swells, the moorage was free. But there were rumours even then that Namu would soon be closed forever.

Its sale in 1991 to a private group seemed to guarantee that Namu would continue as a service centre for pleasure boats, as a land-based fishing resort. There was good news and bad news. Repairs began on the old boardwalks and a few of the buildings, but too much of it was crudely done, with bits of plywood nailed over holes. The docks were still full of seiners and gillnetters, but cruisers were asked for the first time to pay overnight moorage. Unfortunately, they didn't get much in return.

In 1994, there were new rumours on the coast. People were saying the property had reverted to B.C. Packers. We stopped there in mid-summer to see what was going on. There was less dock space, only ring bolts to tie to instead of rails. A barge was loading logs at the old wharf; they were logging behind the community, as though paying for the place by stripping it of its trees.

Up in the village the liquor store was permanently closed, the telephones had been taken away, even the office was gutted and empty. And again there were only empty shelves in the store, a few old vegetables rotting in their bins. We'd arrived just before the supply ship called at Namu, but cruisers familiar with the coast shouldn't expect Namu to still be what it used to be.

Some things will probably never change. There's good water at the dock, the last stop for many before heading into the Hakai wilderness. And a walk up to Namu Lake and its coarse-sand beach is a beautiful way to spend an hour or two. We once found tiny frogs up there, by the hundreds, each one about the size of a honey bee. If the fishing fleet is in, Namu will be quite crowded, and the store may be in short supply at the best of times.

We talked to a fisherman hunkered over a thick salmon sandwich on the deck of his gillnetter. We asked him if the rumours about B.C. Packers were true.

"Well, we've heard that," he said. "But we think it's a lot of B.S."

"There's sure not much left," I said.

"Nothing." He shook his head. "It's like one of those old European cemeteries for dead soldiers."

Milbanke Sound

At Ivory Island the navigator is faced with three choices. The most sheltered route leads north through Reid Passage and up through Mathieson Channel. More exposed is a route west of Ivory Island and north by Milbanke Sound and Finlayson Channel. Either way, they reconnect south of Cone Island; the differences between them are minor.

The third choice takes the navigator twelve miles out toward an open horizon. If he kept going due west, he'd bump into south Moresby Island, a hundred miles away. But if he turns north past McInnes Island, he enters the outer passage at Aristazabal Island.

There's no shelter at all for thirty miles between Seaforth Channel and Aristazabal. Fishermen know a shortcut in the lee of the islands around McInnes, but the passage is harrowing at the least. Fortunately there's a more sheltered route to the outside passage, taking the navigator up to Boat Bluff and then west through Meyers Passage.

But for a southbound trip the thirty-mile crossing becomes a downwind jaunt. We've come this way three times, and arrived at Ivory Island once at dawn, once at mid-day and once at dusk, with a huge whale circling the boat like a dog at a mailman's heels.

Fog often forms in the Sound on summer nights and can linger all day at times. But in clear weather an overnight sail around the bottom of Price Island is a wonderful experience.

Navigators using this route at night should take note of the light characteristics at McInnes and Ivory islands as explained in the *List of Lights*. Both are obscured in broad sweeps; there are other lights on Susan Rock and Idol Point. It's confusing only if you don't know what to expect. We listened one night to a pleasure boat calling the Ivory lightstation for directions when he couldn't find the comforting flash of its beacon.

Boat Bluff

The junction of Tolmie Channel and Meyers Passage is the last chance for a northbound navigator to choose between the inner and outer passages before he reaches Wright Sound.

Most boats will follow the route of the B.C. Ferries, straight up Tolmie and into the channels passing north of Princess Royal Island. Very few boats turn south at Split Head and enter Meyers Passage for the eleven-mile trip to Laredo Sound.

But Meyers Narrows, five miles from Split Head, is nothing like the navigational embolisms found along the southern coast, and pales beside either Seymour or Nakwakto rapids. Like most of the northern narrows, the current is fairly weak; it reaches a maximum of just three knots. The passage can be safely negotiated by any boat with the proper charts.

Meyers Passage leads into Laredo Sound and, though there are obstructions at the entrance, opens immediately into the wide channels stretching north all the way to the top of Banks Island. For boats going south, Meyers Passage offers a chance to head back into sheltered waters if fog or southerly winds hinder a passage down the outside of Price Island.

Klemtu, a little village just south of Split Head, has a fuel dock and store. There is a small post office at the southern end of the community.

Wright Sound

Gil Island, on the south side of Wright Sound, sits like the centre of a huge traffic circle at the confluence of five major passages. North and south, it's the deep-sea route to Kitimat; east and west, it's a connecting link between the narrow channels of the Inside Passage.

Two arms of the interchange reach beyond Campania Island to connect with the outer passage at Nepean Sound and Caamaño Sound. Boats slogging into headwinds on the outer route can turn inland and find immediate shelter east of Campania. Or those weary of the confines of Princess Royal Channel or Grenville Channel can turn west for a change of scenery.

For northbound boats this is the last chance to choose the outer passage before it converges with the Inside Passage at the Skeena River. And there are good reasons for doing just that.

Grenville Channel can be unappealing to boats that are either very small or very slow. There are only three really good anchorages along its forty-five-mile length, and traffic is heavy. We were almost set on the rocks north of Lowe Inlet when we met the *Queen of the North* barrelling through the narrowest gap of the channel, just two cables wide. The ship throws up an enormous wake, and it doesn't slow down.

Principe Channel is just the opposite. It's never less than a mile across, and it's not heavily travelled. Both sides are indented by little bays and long inlets that provide good shelter.

Like all of the dividing points, Wright Sound has a small settlement nearby. Hartley Bay, just north of Promise Island, has limited supplies for the cruiser. A small store operates in a private home—a common practise in the coastal villages. Fuel is usually available, but not always.

Porcher Island

The Inside Passage and the outer route meet off the southeast corner of Porcher Island. For northbound boats there isn't much choice: you go straight up Ogden Channel toward Prince Rupert. But heading south you choose here between the convenience of Grenville Channel and the wilderness of the various passages to the west.

The easiest way to connect to Principe Channel is through Ogden and Petrel channels, using the tide to carry you south. But Kitkatla Inlet is just a few hours out of the way, an enchanting place for those with time to go exploring.

Two communities are tucked away in this area. Oona River, on the southeast corner of Porcher Island, has no provisions for cruising boats. Two mooring buoys lie off the entrance, for the use of boats waiting for a high tide to let them slip over the shoals. Tide height is marked on a scale on the pilings. Kitkatla, on the north side of Dolphin Island, has a small store in a private home, but no fuel is available.

≈ THE ANCHORAGES ≈

These charts are intended as references only. They should give the boater an idea of what a place is like, of what to expect when he gets there. But they are definitely **NOT TO BE USED FOR NAVIGATION!** For that reason, they contain neither depths nor contours, nor precise positions of submerged hazards.

Though I have tried to make them as accurate as possible, they cannot take the place of the National Hydrographic Service charts referenced after the name of each anchorage.

As we return to these places ourselves, it will be with the real charts for navigation.

≈ 1 ≈
SCHOONER RETREAT

chart 3934/3779

We didn't have much luck with weather the first time we crossed Queen Charlotte Sound on our way south to Port Hardy. It was cold and rainy, and the wind was always from the south. So we approached the Sound in little steps—from Namu to Goldstream Harbour to Safety Cove—hoping for at least a wind shift before we hit the open water. And then we reached Schooner Retreat and had nowhere to go that would take us any closer.

We chose Frigate Bay, drawn by the reassuring name of the passage—"Safe Entrance"—and sat with a stern line to the little Fire Islets. There was a small jewel of a beach on Ironside Island, at the west side of Frigate Bay.

Even in the cold rain and southeast wind, we were entranced by the little bays of Penrose Island. There were lovely pocket beaches, scores of birds, and the sound of the surf on the outer rocks. But we were in a hurry that year, and left as soon as we saw the blue hummocks of Vancouver Island faintly in the distance.

It was sooner than we should have, for the sky socked in again as soon as we passed Kelp Head, and we didn't see another bit of land at all for almost twelve hours. We shouldered through the waves of a mounting southeaster, watching the clock and the compass, leaning forward like bicyclists as though that would speed us on our way. When the land finally loomed out

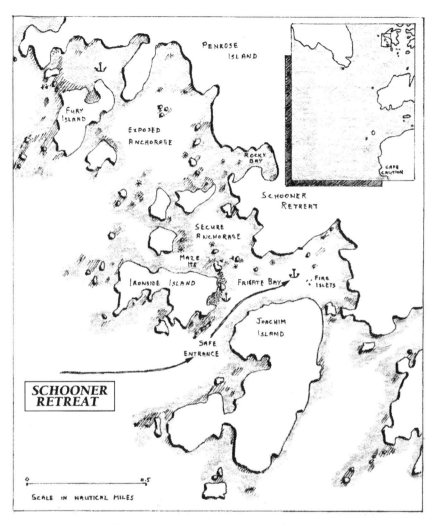

SCHOONER
RETREAT

SCALE IN NAUTICAL MILES

of the rain and fog, it didn't look at all like Pine Island. And no
wonder: we were off Roller Bay, six miles to the west.

We would have been wiser to have waited a little longer at
Schooner Retreat. And we would have been a lot more comfortable.
There's no pleasure in rushing up and down the coast from place
to place, and we'd gone hurrying through its most beautiful parts
like passengers on a non-stop bus, without seeing a thing.

It was five years before I returned to Schooner Retreat, with
my brother instead of Kristin, and in the interval the place had
become a park and had been "discovered" by the cruising fleet.

Little boats from the lodges of Rivers Inlet trolled along the
fifty-fathom line off the surf of Rouse Reef. Sailboats and
motoryachts filled the shallow bay north of Exposed Anchorage,

tucked in there behind long, white-shell beaches and before a row of old dolphins. But Frigate Bay was empty still, and we anchored just inside Safe Entrance off a lovely arc of golden sand on the corner of Ironside Island. At low tide, the island connected to the small islets to the south over vast fields of broken shell, great huge heaps that slithered and clattered under our boots like slopes of shale.

I took my brother's kayak north through the Maze Islets, out beyond the logged-off bluffs of Ironside Island, to off-lying reefs thick with seabirds. Each one, as I passed, exploded into squawking, feathery balls that tumbled down from stony shelves and poured like lemmings into the sea. The small, grey birds didn't fly away, but paddled through the surf streaming tiny wakes behind them.

Schooner Retreat, now part of the spectacular 2,000-hectare Penrose Island Marine Park, includes a number of separate anchorages. Only three of them are named: Frigate Bay, Secure Anchorage and Exposed Anchorage. The *Sailing Directions for the B.C. Coast* has this to say: "During SE and SW gales the gusts are furious in these anchorages, but with good ground tackle and care there is no danger in Schooner Retreat."

≈ 2 ≈
SAFETY COVE

chart 3727/3934

Safety cove has been the traditional spot for generations of mariners waiting out fog or bad weather before making a southward crossing of Queen Charlotte Sound. It's also, for many boaters going north, the first anchorage they'll see beyond Cape Caution. But Safety Cove is not the only choice in the immediate area, and far from the most attractive.

Loggers were carving out the northern shore in the summer of 1994, working the high slopes with two skidders and a huge, orange machine. A booming ground sprawled well into the bay, and the noise echoed through the hills from dawn to sunset.

Safety Cove is deep far into the bay, then shelves rapidly to a vast drying flat of gooey mud and boulders. Winds funnel down through the valley at its head and seem stronger in the anchorage sometimes than they do outside. On a typical summer night, pleasure boats form a fan at the head of the bay while fishboats anchor further out.

Our favourite spot is on the southern shore, just before the bay shallows in mats of weed. There's a small indent there, a splotch of blue on the chart. The holding, in thirty to forty feet, is as good as anywhere in the cove, and it seems that winds pouring out of the hills don't blow quite as hard along this shore. The steep cliffs at the back of the niche are covered with sea life, but there's an old wreck in the corner, a boat of about

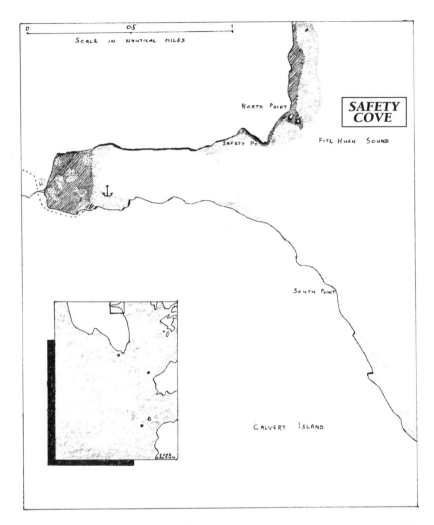

forty feet lying southeast to northwest, so caution is needed. We found ourselves almost on top of it once, looking down at a gaping hatch and twisted bow. Parts of the wreck were exposed on a tide height of two feet.

Though extensive flats would discourage the Little People from landing at Safety Cove, a good-sized stream drains into its head. And a system of old mining roads offers a route into the hills of lower Calvert Island. Once you're through the tangles above the beach, it's a pleasant walk among streams and bogs, and an abandoned settlement is supposed to lie somewhere along the fading maze of roadbeds. A trail begins on the south shore of Safety Cove, on an old landing flagged by tape. Try to land on a rising tide; even here the mud flats are a bit formidable.

*Above the mud flats of
Safety Cove, the beach
is strewn with rocks and
a few enormous
boulders.*

At least the fishing is good at Safety Cove. Salmon were leaping and splashing throughout the bay in the summer of '94, and skiffs from the fancy lodges of Hakai came south to troll across the mouth of the anchorage. They jostled like square dancers, promenading back and forth between Safety Point and North Point.

For someone just looking for a place to stop and sleep after a day of travelling, Safety Cove is a convenient spot. But it can be quite uncomfortable when wind and swells come from different directions. And there are plenty of alternatives among the little nooks and crannies only a few miles away on the eastern shore of Fitz Hugh Sound.

Our favourite is Schooner Retreat.

≈ 3 ≈
KWAKSHUA CHANNEL

chart 3784

K wakshua Channel separates Calvert Island from Hecate Island. From Fitz Hugh Sound, it runs straight west for nearly five miles, then makes a right-angle turn to the north. But a westward extension of the channel bulges into a three-armed anchorage that reaches, in two places, within a mile of the open sea and creates a little knob at the northwest tip of Calvert Island.

The anchorage is Pruth Bay. We used to aim for it the day we left home, wandering nearly three hundred miles just to be there, to sit on beaches that shook with surf, to watch the night fall over an empty ocean. We'd pick berries on the trails, catch squid in the harbour, find wonderful treasures stranded on lonely shores. When the Hakai Recreation Area was created, encompassing, as just a tiny part, Pruth Bay and its surrounding beaches, we were wonderfully pleased. Though boats flocked there by the dozen, there was lots of room for everyone.

We met a group of businessmen there one year. They were staying in a little cabin tucked among the trees: sports fishing, they said. And when they came to us for help, desperate to make phone calls and long-distance deals, we gladly offered them a radio.

Now I'm terrified that we helped destroy Pruth Bay. For within months the land was sold to private developers, and within a year the place was ruined. The little cabin in the woods was stripped away; even the woods were stripped away. And a

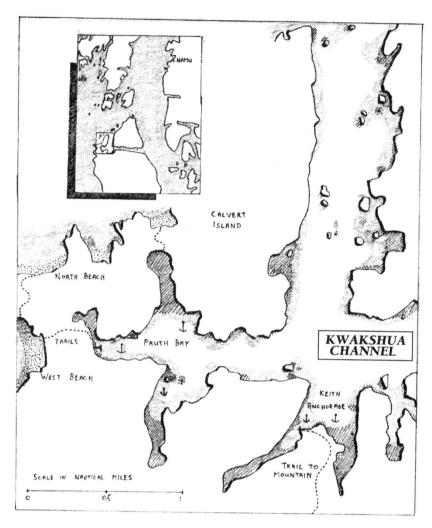

huge fishing resort sprang up on the beach above the harbour. "A park within a park" they called it, and put in a skeet-shooting range, a place for golfers to practise, a hot tub made of fake rock. They built a monstrous dock and armed it with loudspeakers that broadcast fishermen's boasts through the anchorage. And then, still not satisfied, they started gouging and tearing at the forest behind it. They built a road across the peninsula; they lit it at night with fake lanterns.

And that was it for us. We said we'd never go back to Pruth Bay.

Apparently, we weren't alone. In the summer of 1994, we found only three yachts in an anchorage that used to fill nightly with so many boats you could hardly row a dinghy between them. The floating information building, a park headquarters, was still moored to the rock at the side of the bay, but no one was there, and no one was visiting. And that was the saddest thing of all.

It's a tragedy that developers got their grubby hands on this little tract of private land. But it would be even worse if cruisers wiped Kwakshua Channel from their list of places to go.

There isn't much appeal anymore in the main anchorage of Pruth Bay. Debris from the fishing operation goes straight in the water. But fortunately there are several alternatives to the over-used west arm with its view now of red roofs and glass walls. The north arm, where we anchored once and watched otter babies get a lesson in sea-urchin fishing, is the least used, though it dries very quickly just inside the entrance. A trail connects from its head to the beaches of Choked Passage. All sorts of treasures wash ashore there: we found a plastic armchair tossed up in a rocky cleft, a picnic cooler with three cans of beer still inside it, still cold. I thought I'd never been luckier, until I had to find enough space in a crowded sailboat to stow a full-sized armchair. It reached out its arms like a cat, and grabbed at every bulkhead and table top.

The south arm of Pruth Bay, though, is the nicer spot, with good anchorage behind the small islet at its western edge. The bay should be entered well toward its eastern shore, for a long reef connects the islet to the west side and continues halfway across the entrance. The wind can sometimes blow quite strongly through the valleys to the south.

Until a few years ago, there was a house on the point inside Keith Anchorage, just to the east of Pruth Bay. This was the home of caretakers for the B.C. Tel microwave station atop the hill behind it. The house is gone, but a rutted road leads up to the towers and the big windmills that generate power. The view is fantastic.

Both of the inlets extending from the anchorage dry out on low tides. We've anchored off the house site, right on the edge of the drying flats, and off the remains of the old dock at the entrance to the other inlet. A strong current sweeps out from there on the ebb tide; a good place to suspend the boat between two anchors. The road begins at the dockhead and passes close by an old cedar tree that had planks split from its side long ago. Just beyond it a side trail—nearly obscured now by thick bushes—drops downhill to a nice little beach behind the flattened house foundations. The caretakers used to feed by hand the wolves that roam through the muskeg hills, but now large flocks of geese gather in long grass behind the beach.

The *Sailing Directions* offers this warning: "Anchorage can be obtained midway between the entrance points of Keith Anchorage in 11 fathoms (20 metres). This anchorage is reported to be unsafe in SE gales because of heavy squalls that funnel down the valleys at its head."

Fishing lodges have settled in several bays in the area, booming off once-useful anchorages, barring access to the better streams in a place where drinking water can sometimes be hard to find. But a few small creeks empty down the north shore of Kwakshua Channel, and we've filled our barrels there, then carefully boiled every drop.

≈ 4 ≈
ADAMS HARBOUR

chart 3784

We came south one year down Kildidt Sound and crossed Hakai Passage in a cold drizzle. We hadn't seen the sun for days, and the wind was always against us, whatever course we took. Late in the afternoon we poked into Adams Harbour only to find it small and claustrophobic. There was a fishcamp's boom stretched across a big chunk of the anchorage, a sign in the trees almost begging people not to leave garbage behind. So we turned east, and snuck in through the bottom of Rattenbury Island on the rising tide.

Maybe it was the weather that day, our moods drenched by a week of rain, but we'd skirted one of the most attractive spots in the Hakai area, and given it barely a glance. It wasn't until the next year that we went all the way in to the top of Choked Passage, and found a beautiful harbour waiting for us at the very tip of Calvert Island.

There were sailboats anchored here and there, a couple of big charter boats webbed into convenient clefts. Someone had found himself a lonely spot in the narrow gap between Starfish and Odlum islands, though he seemed to be having a rather rough time of it with the swell surging in and out. But the water was clear and calm, and it rippled against long sweeps of sandy beach. We anchored behind Starfish Island, then anchored again when the tidal current came sweeping in with a force that surprised us.

"It is known locally as Welcome Harbour. Though confined, this

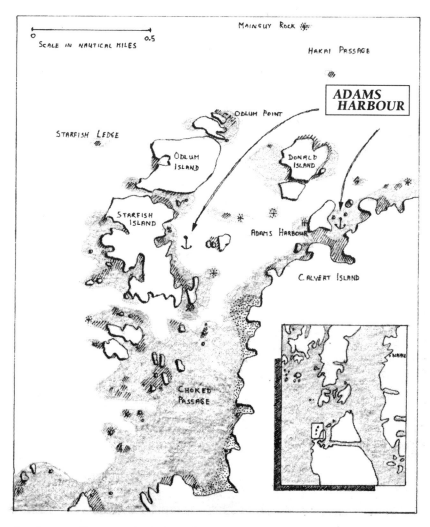

harbour offers good shelter for small vessels from all but strong west winds, which send a swell into the harbour. Local knowledge is advised for entering the harbour." (The *Sailing Directions*)

But on our second visit, we saw a sailboat plucked from its anchor in strong south winds. It went scudding through the harbour, veering and tilting in the gusts, and a knot of fishing skiffs swarmed around it like wasps. All we could do was watch; we were webbed firmly into the cleft halfway up the eastern shore of Starfish Island, suspended in the middle with lines to each shore. A large charter boat had moored there in previous years, leaving behind a ring bolt drilled through the rock, a scattering of burnt garbage. And though the wind peaked at more than twenty knots, we felt hardly a breath in there.

We explored the harbour by dinghy and kayak, found little beaches with no footprints at all. Apart from a shortage of fresh water—and a steady stream of floatplane traffic—the shores of Odlum Harbour are perfect for the Little People.

The largest beach in the harbour is used each summer by members of a private fishing club, the Hakai Land and Sea Society. Their camp is tucked unobtrusively among the trees and bushes above the sand, but its presence tends to discourage visitors. Though no one came out to chase us off the beach, we still felt almost like trespassers on this bit of Hakai park.

But it's a minor complaint. Adams Harbour is a huge place, and there's always another beach just around the corner.

The Marabell

The anchor was dragging. I could feel the vibrations, as it bounced along the bottom, ringing up through the nylon rode between my hands. Kristin, in the cockpit, put the engine in gear and motored slowly ahead against the tide. And the skiff came by then, a little yellow boat with a name across the bow: *Marabell*. There was one person inside.

He wore a squashed down Tilly hat—his lucky hat, probably— and his fishing rods lay on the thwarts, tip to tip like dueling swords. He puttered past the bow and looked up at me. "Nice to see a double-ender," he said.

I was pulling in the line hand over hand, letting it pile at my feet. I'd made a bad mistake anchoring across the current. And I smiled down at him as the anchor jarred and bounced; he was a nice old man.

"What is she?" he said. "Thirty-two?"

I shook my head. The shoreline was passing the wrong way, the boat swinging in the current. I felt the deck shudder as Kristin pushed on the throttle. "Twenty-seven," I said. He really was a nice old man. But I wished he'd go away.

"That so?" he said, and gave a little laugh.

The first links of chain came rattling over the roller. I felt the anchor lift, hang there, three times its normal weight in a thick clot of weeds.

"She looks bigger," said the nice old man.

Kristin grunted. "We're trying to re-anchor," she said. "We've got a bit of a situation."

The man nodded at her. He smiled and said, "I've got a double-ender too."

Donald Lawrence launches his kayak in the surf at Adams Harbour.

He was still talking as we motored on ahead of him, swung round to anchor again behind Starfish Island. Then he just drifted off, and puttered away in his yellow skiff.

We came to know the boat, saw it everywhere. And it took us quite a while to realize there was actually a whole fleet of identical yellow boats, because each time we saw one, we looked quickly away.

They were pretty little boats, like songbirds as they trolled among the Boston Whalers of the fancy lodges. They came and went from the *Marabell*, a large white-hulled ship anchored by the shore of Adams Harbour, moored to the rocks there. They belonged together, these old-time skiffs and the picturesque *Marabell*, a one-time warship.

She started life as the *YMS88*, a minesweeper built in the U.S. navy yards of California's bay area. Commissioned three months after the attack on Pearl Harbour, she finished the war credited with sinking one submarine.

Converted to a peace-time yacht, she went through several owners until she was eventually bought by Dr. Ballard, the pet-food king. Apparently, he intended to hunt seals and put them in cans. But his plan was never realized, and the old *YMS88* became a survey vessel for the Canadian Hydrographic Service.

In the early seventies, she was sold again, and finally converted to a yacht for fishing charters. Under her present owner, Bob Wright of Undersea Gardens, the *Marabell* has been working each summer near Hakai Passage for more than a dozen years.

Where a crew of fifty U.S. sailors once lived and worked, groups of twenty to twenty-three guests stay in private cabins, gather in a common lounge. They fly in and out by floatplane from Vancouver, fish the nearby waters in *Marabell*'s bright yellow skiffs. In the evenings, they spread out plastic lawn chairs on the foredeck, where a naval gun once guarded the sea lanes of the Pacific Ocean.

Captain Mike Robinson, his engineer, and the fish master, all live in cabins added to the upper deck. They seem proud of their vessel's history; the boat herself seems proud. *Marabell* still has her original engines, and guests can trace her several incarnations through years of conversions and renovations.

≈ 5 ≈
SPIDER ANCHORAGE

chart 3784

I f you visit the parks staff at their building in Pruth Bay, they will give you a map that shows the best beaches and camping spots among the islands and inlets of Kildidt Sound. They might even twist your arm a bit, in an effort to persuade you to visit this central portion of the vast and beautiful Hakai Recreation Area. They did that to us, and we didn't regret it for a moment.

A school of porpoises escorted us up the Sound, and we spent a few days in the area, then kept on going along the outer coast: around Superstition Point and up through Cultus Sound, Sans Peur Passage, and Hunter Channel to Bella Bella. Now it seems that more and more boaters are using Kildidt Sound and the whole Hakai Recreation Area as a destination in itself. We found several boats anchored among the islands of Spider Anchorage and down through the Breadner Group that first year, several more the next year, and again the year after.

Spider Anchorage, in the midst of a group of islands separating Kildidt and Queens Sound, can be approached from four directions. In the north, Spider Channel passes through a cluster of small islets, but the route is sheltered and easy to follow. Fulton Passage, in the west, is wide and clear, but exposed to westerly winds. The eastern route passes either north or south of the Kittyhawk Group and winds past the southern tip of Hurri-

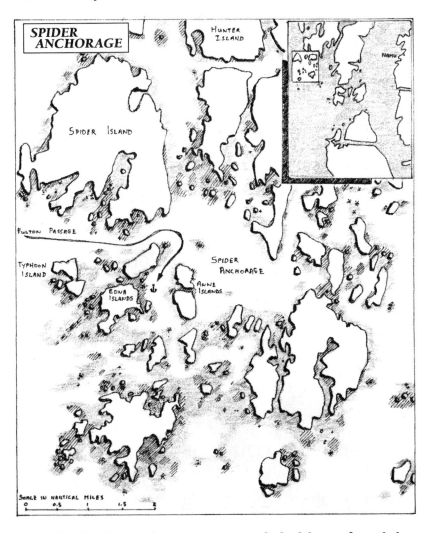

cane Island. The southern entrance is choked by reefs and drying rocks, but offers the shortest route from Hakai Passage.

From any direction, the islands surrounding Spider Anchorage provide good shelter in countless nooks and coves. There's one tiny bay, ringed by islets, where a little cabin sits above the prettiest beach you could hope to find. There's a clearing for a tent and a little trickle of water. But you'll have to find it for yourself; we've been sworn to secrecy.

A good choice is the little bay off the eastern shore of the Edna Islands. On days of westerly winds, a mist of spray drifts inland through the gap. But boats are sheltered in the bay below it, and the place can sometimes be quite crowded. At low tide, we carried the dinghy over the drying spit, and rowed out to

Walking in the rain on the west side of the Edna Islands. The beaches are steep and exposed.

Typhoon Island, right on the edge of Queens Sound.

It's a rocky shore out there, the trees all driven back by the sea, the cliffs like balding stone foreheads. And between them, behind lines of jagged reefs, beaches and coves, collect masses of logs rough-sanded by the sea. It's a hard walk to scramble along that shoreline. But we were rewarded by finding one small glass ball that had somehow drifted over that rock and landed high among the scrub bushes on the shore.

My brother and I spent ten days anchored in little bays just one-island's width from Queens Sound, both north and south of Hakai Passage. Then we rounded Superstition Point and anchored in an inland cove off Sans Peur Passage. We turned off the engine and just stood on deck, wondering what was wrong.

"It's sure quiet," my brother said.

And that was it. We'd grown so used to the sound of surf that it thundered now, silently, in our ears.

≈ 6 ≈
GOOSE ISLANDS

chart 3786/3728

One year we put in a lot of effort getting to the Goose Islands. They sit offshore, like lonely outposts, and everything we'd heard about them made them seem like enchanted islands, seldom visited and thick with seabirds.

We came at them from the north, waiting endlessly in the midst of the Tribal Group for a break in the steady rain and an appearance of the long-forecast westerlies. We could see the islands, low and hazy in the distance, and dreamed of long, sandy beaches where we'd find no footprints and hundreds of glass balls.

We'd been there three days when a family in an older cabin cruiser came in and anchored near us. They brought us a huge slab of fresh cod.

"So you're going to the Goose Islands?" said the man. He looked up at the sky. "You won't want to be out there if it blows southeast. The tide gushes out of Raymond Passage and Hunter Channel. With an opposing wind," he said, "it kicks up into a vicious chop.

"You can't run back; it's dangerous," he said. "And you can't stay there; there's no shelter." He shook his head. "No, you don't want to be there in a southeaster."

When the radio promised northerly winds, we slipped across to Goose Island Anchorage, seven miles away, as the sky turned from grey to blue. The water was so clear I could watch the

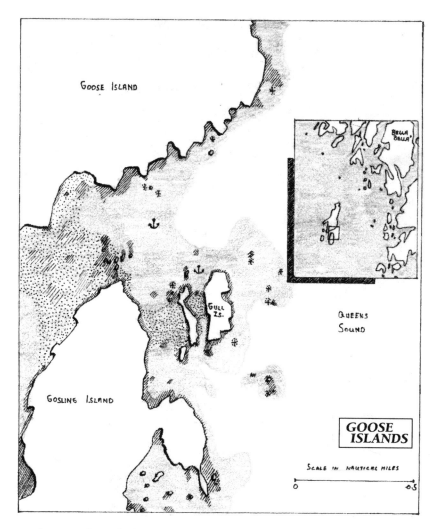

anchor set four fathoms down. On every side, sand beaches glistened in the sun. And boats had come from everywhere.

To the right, a group of hunters was stepping ashore from an aluminum skiff. To the left, a kayaker was setting up camp on his private beach. Ahead, three boats sat at anchor, and one big charter operator had put up tents on the main beach.

We were surprised, even more so as the tide rose and the beaches sank, one by one. At high tide, there was a broad gap between Goose Island and Gosling Island. And in the morning, the forecast called for southeast winds, rising to gale force overnight.

We'd spent so much time just getting there that we decided to stay and ride out whatever came our way. The other boats left, the kayaker packed up and paddled away, and we settled down alone as the first clouds came scudding darkly up from the south. In slickers and boots, we went for a walk along the beach. In places the sand was soft as snow; we'd sink into it nearly to our boot tops. But much of what we'd thought would be unspoiled beaches of golden sand turned out to be fields of thick gravel and fist-sized rocks. There were no glass balls, but lots of footprints. Still we weren't completely disappointed; it really was a beautiful and mysterious place.

By late afternoon the sky was a dark, dark blue. A swell was rolling into the anchorage, and the air had that heavy, oppressive feel of a coming storm. We re-set the anchors, and waited as the boat rocked and rolled.

Just before sunset, a burst of light came piercing through the clouds, making big squares on the water, long trapezoids across the sky. And we saw the sun, briefly, a bright and promising red. There'd be no gale that night, despite the forecast.

≈ 7 ≈

THE TRIBAL GROUP

chart 3786/3787

On a southbound trip, the Tribal Group sits at a convenient place to wait for favourable weather before heading on to the Hakai Recreation Area.

A long, slender lake in the middle of Iroquois Island drains to the north through a steep cut in the shore. The water is good, and easily accessible; animal trails wind through the trees toward the lake. Here, where two small islands form a sheltered elbow, we tied a shore line to a yew tree and explored the group by dinghy.

I wrote in our log: "A strong current ebbs through here, over a series of drying bars out to Queens Sound. Found a pod of killer whales swimming in the next bay over."

At low tide, an interesting series of beaches appears along the west coast of Iroquois Island. The little islets off its shore, and Huron Island to the west, are wind-blown and wild. We saw porpoises here as well as killer whales, and in tidepools an incredible variety of little creatures.

The *Sailing Directions* recommends that boaters use Codfish Passage or Safe Passage when transiting between Queens Sound and Raymond Passage. We went south through the gap between Iroquois and Athabaskan islands, a route that the *Pilot* says should not be used without local knowledge. The tidal stream can be very strong, and certainly requires careful reading of the

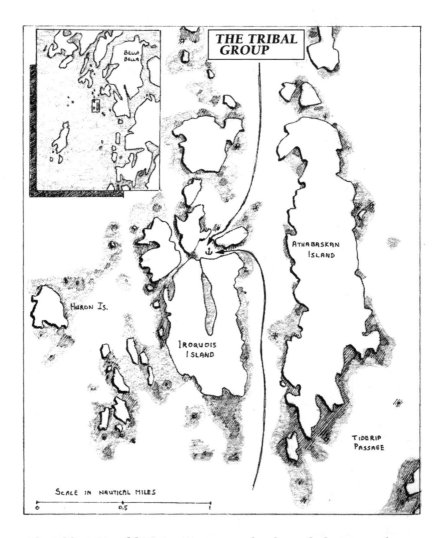

THE TRIBAL GROUP

BELLA BELLA

ATHABASKAN ISLAND

HERON Is.

IROQUOIS ISLAND

TIDE RIP PASSAGE

SCALE IN NAUTICAL MILES
0   0.5   1

tide tables. In addition, numerous shoals and drying rocks extend beyond both ends and across the centre of the channel. Be careful of the outgoing tide: it tries very hard to put you onto the rocks off the south tip of Iroquois Island.

A better route, perhaps, would involve backtracking three miles north to Codfish Passage.

≈ 8 ≈
LIZZIE COVE

chart 3785/3787

W here Lama Passage meets Hunter Channel and swings north to Bella Bella, Cooper Inlet provides pleasant anchorages in a series of four coves: Ada, Jane, Fanny and Lizzie.

Though we've spent several nights and whole days in the inlet, both Ada and Jane are strangers to us. We've anchored off the mouth of Fanny Cove by a steep beach across from Gus Island, where the tide came surging over our campfire. It swept away a fork and a plate, but uncovered a bread knife that some-one else had lost. Further in, we've anchored behind the row of drying rocks forming a shallow bight just south and west of the entrance narrows. The streams that feed into Fanny were won-derfully warm, and we set out along a trail up the river's north bank until it vanished into the bush a short way upstream.

But of the four sister coves forming Cooper Inlet, it's Lizzie—plump and inviting—who attracts the sailors. Particularly when the wind is from the northwest.

"Small craft can obtain secure anchorage in 7 to 9 fathoms (13 to 17 metres) in the middle of Lizzie Cove," says the *Sailing Directions*, "but local knowledge is advised because of rocks in the entrance."

"Too cautious," I said, and went straight in past Hogan Rock and through the deep-water passage shown on the chart. We spent one night in the cove, then left the same way in the morn-

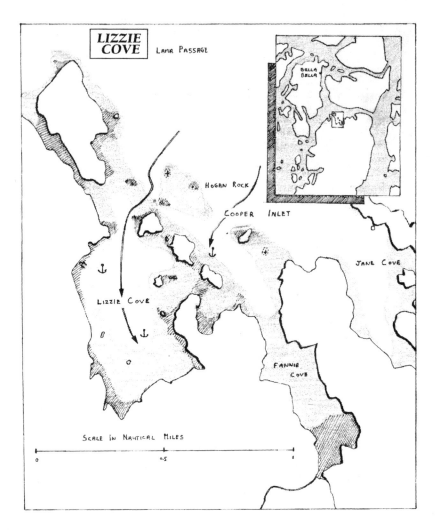

ing. Kristin stood on the bow, watching for rocks—wasting her time, I thought—and broke suddenly into a weird dance on the bowsprit. She'd scared me like that before, bursting into isometric exercises there, moving her shoulders in circles, swinging back on the forestay. But this time she waved her arms and cried, "Stop! Stop!"

I shoved the engine into reverse, trying to halt two tons of boat with a bit of metal the size of a pinwheel. And with a shudder that ran from keel to masthead, we plowed into the biggest underwater rock we'd ever seen. Kristin went below to look for water seeping in. She was back in a moment. "It's knee-deep down there," she said. And laughed. "Just kidding."

It seems the rock is an underwater extension of the large islet at the harbour's mouth. We didn't see it at all the second time we stopped at Lizzie Cove, when we swung well into the centre of the channel. And this time, instead of anchoring in the main harbour, we turned left at the entrance and found a beautiful spot among the scattered islets. There were ruins of a crude structure on one, a flagpole on another, and a small beach of shell and gravel that only flooded on a tide of thirteen feet.

"You've found the perfect anchorage," said a sailor from another boat. He paddled past in a kayak, looking for remains of the Icelandic settlement that once flourished in the harbour. On the beach he'd found a bit of carved bone; so Lizzie Cove has been a busy place, from prehistoric times right to the present—homesteaders still live on the southwest shore.

On our first visit to the cove, we thought we'd stumbled onto a stone man laid out on the beach. It was a morning thick with fog, and I kept seeing patterns in the stones. When the fog broke, suddenly, I was standing in a man's head, looking straight down the body toward the sun between his feet. I called Kristin over, showed her the circular face, the arms and legs as crude as a kindergarten drawing. "Then those must be his shoes," she said, pointing to odd mounds of rock. And she laughed. "It's just a bunch of rocks."

But I rowed out to the boat, fetched back the hand-bearing compass, a measuring tape and pencils. And we plotted the stone man onto a notebook page.

"Well, you've left out half the rocks," said Kristin. "I really think you're getting carried away."

"Maybe," I said. "This is probably how Erich von Däniken got his start."

≈ 9 ≈

THE TRAP

chart 3785

Two miles south of Lama Passage, Clayton Island forms a sheltered little passage on the west shore of Fisher Channel. On the chart it looks like a highway pull-off, a little rest stop where you might find green-walled toilets and litter bins chained to the pavement. It's not a great anchorage; the channel's steep and rock-bottomed. But we've tucked ourselves in there several times—always with a shore line to keep us from swinging—once at the north end and twice at the south, off the place that's called The Trap. It's a broad, circular indent in the shore. At high tide, it looks like an inviting anchorage. At low tide, it empties like a washbasin.

For years, we accepted the common belief that the name is a little joke on boats that have found themselves in there with more draught than water. But one day we walked over the dried-out flats and found a labyrinth of stone walls and silted trenches. It was one of the best examples we've seen of the ancient fish traps that were once used to harvest salmon.

There were so many fish at one time that traps could be built anywhere along the shore. In places, salmon would find their way into the traps themselves, in others they'd be herded in by fishermen thrashing at the water with cedar boughs. Either way, as the tide fell the salmon would be trapped among the stone walls and scooped up for the harvest.

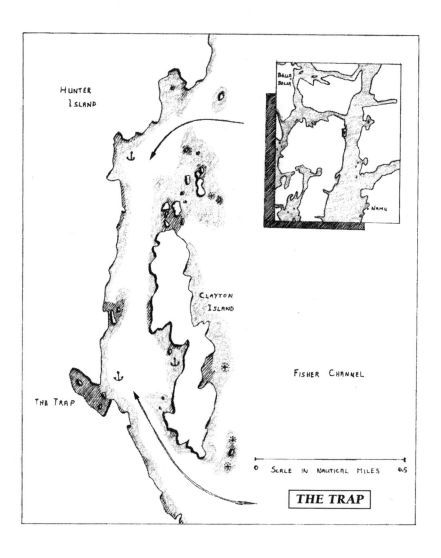

HUNTER
ISLAND

BELLA
BELLA

NAMU

CLAYTON
ISLAND

FISHER CHANNEL

THE TRAP

0   SCALE IN NAUTICAL MILES   0.5

THE TRAP

A rising tide outlines the natural islands and man-made walls of The Trap.

It's interesting to sit on the islet in the centre of The Trap and watch the tide flood in around you. It pours into the pools and dams up against the ancient walls, outlining their curves and gates. It pushes back the stream water and surges in behind the island from both directions. On a tide of fourteen feet, we could row the dinghy over the last of the walls and drift across the shallows.

In recent years a hand-logger has been working on Clayton Island across from The Trap, booming logs in its central bight. But in the summer of 1994, the logger had moved on and we anchored in his place, in the spot shown on the chart as nine-feet deep. We sat very close to shore, but still had thirty feet under the keel on a seven-foot tide. It's the best anchorage in the area, and the change in scenery from high tide to low tide is particularly dramatic.

≈ 10 ≈
LONG POINT COVE

There's an old boat shed in Long Point Cove, an interesting place just south of Pointer Island. Sometimes gloomy, the cove is closed in and darkens early. But all night, the occulting light on Pointer Island flashes through the mouth and across the trees, over and over, four seconds on, two seconds off. On a foggy night, with the horn blasting just eight cables away, the effect is quite stunning.

"Long Point Cove is an excellent anchorage for small craft," says the *Sailing Directions*. "A drying rock lies in the entrance to the cove, about 0.2 mile north of Long Point."

Deeper in, the cove widens by the old boat shed. There's another rock in the middle, bits of boom chain and rusted cable here and there. We haven't snagged the anchor, but I imagine it could happen, and an anchor buoy might be a wise precaution.

It was interesting to poke through the lean-to shed. We wondered over a crude steam box, the little bits and pieces left behind: homemade tools, a clutch of leg-hold traps, scraps of planking and sawn-off mast sections, wadded magazines.

"Maybe he built his boat and sailed away," said Kristin.

I hoped so. I imagined him at night, sitting all alone by a fire and reading his magazines by the four-second flash of the Pointer Island light.

The shoal around Walbran Rock is an excellent fishing spot.

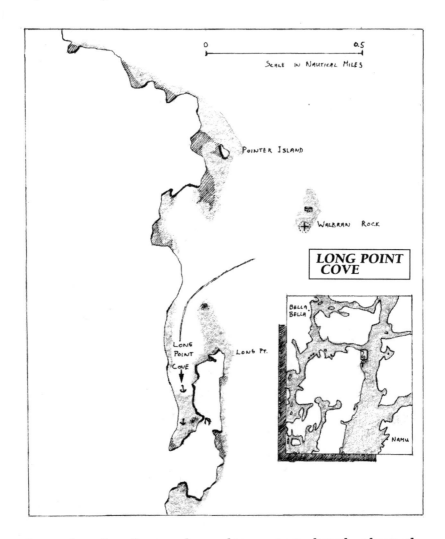

Remember that the can buoy does not sit directly above the rock, but north and west of it. And watch for the tidal stream; it can run very strongly over the shallows.

If there's a gillnet opening in Fisher Channel, you may find extra nets stored in skiffs moored in the cove.

Kristin found Long Point Cove a lot less appealing than I did. She remembers it as "slippery, dank, and smelling of mold." I like it for its quiet and loneliness, but recent logging has spoiled some of its charm.

≈ 11 ≈
KISAMEET BAY

chart 3785

Kisameet Bay is a shallow, protected bight on the eastern shore of Fisher Channel. Just seven miles north of Namu, it's a good alternative in fishing season to a night at the crowded docks.

Behind the group of islands at its northern end, Kisameet Bay forms a quiet lagoon where an old cabin sits on a rocky islet thick with bushes. To the west, narrow passages look out on Fisher Channel; to the east, Kisameet Lake drains into the bay through a fast-moving river spaced by falls. A good walking trail begins at its mouth on the southern bank just above a wonderful, kidney-shaped fish trap. The trail goes right to the lake, giving spectacular glimpses of the stream below. And throughout the lagoon, the water is fairly shallow, and well sheltered.

It's a spot discovered by the Little People. They've established a camp on a mossy bank just south of the river in a cove above a tiny beach.

Kisameet Bay is best entered south of Kipling Island. But a narrow passage follows the southern shore of the next large island up the bay, passing between it and the small islet north of Kipling Island. By either route several submerged and drying rocks lie within the bay and call for close attention. The dangers are shown clearly on chart 3785.

Kisameet Bay is often used by seine boats between fisheries.

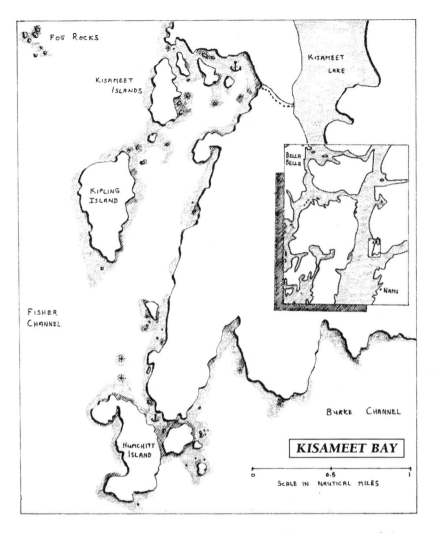

The fishermen, on their days at rest, pass their time spin-fishing from the railings.

We've also anchored at the very southern end of Kisameet Bay in the gap along the northeast shore of Humchitt Island. It's a confined spot, a shallow basin of golden sand. Though more scenic than the north end, it's nowhere near as good an anchorage. When the tide floods the spits of land at its head, the gap opens to the tidal streams of Burke Channel.

≈ 12 ≈
CODVILLE LAGOON

chart 3785

There's a narrow passage connecting Lagoon Bay on the east side of Fisher Channel to the sheltered water of Codville Lagoon. The current can run with some force, and the *Sailing Directions* warns that a rock with less than six feet over it lies slightly north of mid-channel. Pass it on the south side.

Codville Lagoon is a B.C. provincial park. Codville Island, like a tiny cutout of the whole lagoon, sits in the middle. Most boats head straight for the indent in the southeast corner, where an ancient swim float seems to drift from place to place on its mooring. Right at the head, a trail leads up to Sagar Lake.

Marked by a board cracked in two and a red band circling a tree, the trail is steep in places and sometimes rough and muddy. There are sections of old boardwalk remaining from the park's heyday as a recreation spot for residents of Ocean Falls. Though the trail is in sad decline, a hike to Sagar Lake is well worth the effort. Glacial sand of a peculiar strawberry-blond colour forms a long beach across the lake's south shore. The shallow water warms quickly in summer sun, then chills rapidly as it deepens. There are a number of crude campsites cleared in the bushes above the beach, but the area suffers badly from a lack of any facilities. There are wads of old toilet paper everywhere you walk.

Anchorage is good within the inner bay of Codville Lagoon. As the centre shows depths to fifteen fathoms, boats tend to nestle

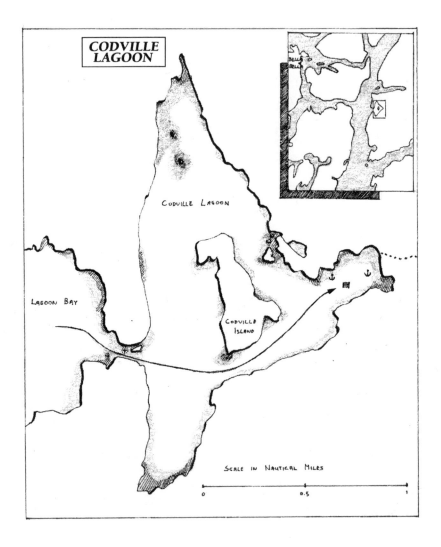

We came across a canoe on the long beach across the bottom of Sagar Lake.

close to shore along the indents on the north side, below ancient forests with great stands of dead, white-trunked trees.

There's a tiny cove behind a fang of reefs, barely room for one boat, another indent just to the east. Boats anchored here seem to vanish into the landscape.

We thought we had the whole lagoon to ourselves when we went ashore on Codville Island for a bear-free barbecue of pork chops from the Namu store. There was no beach to speak of, so we built a fire among a scattering of boulders. We tossed some potatoes into the coals, then sat back as the tide rose. Our firewood floated off, along with one of our boots. Kristin looked sadly at the still-pink chops. "The potatoes will be ready when the Thermos goes under," she said.

At sunset the seals came out. And the dog started barking, first at them and then at her own echo. She barked and yipped and howled. And out of the empty anchorage, faint from distance, came a tiny voice: "Shut that dog up!"

≈ 13 ≈
CYPRESS ISLAND

chart 3720/3785

Every night the boats fill the dock at Shearwater. They line both sides of the long spit of private wharf, then raft up two and three deep. Sailboats, motoryachts, fishboats; they all gather here.

"It's free moorage," a sailor told us, a gleam of avarice in his eye. He was a very big sailor, on a very small boat, and he had a six-pack of beer floating on a tether, his inflatable rolled upside down to keep out the rain. It looked as though he'd been there a while; he didn't seem in any hurry to leave.

He might have strolled ashore that evening, maybe walked through the clutter of the shipyard lot. Then he'd crawl into his bunk and close the hatch against the noise, and fall asleep in the reek of fuel oil and sour mud.

And less than two miles away—he could have been there in half an hour—we sat on a pebbly beach, with a little fire at our feet and mounds of wood at our fingertips. We sat and watched the water turn from blue to red to indigo as the sun set behind us over Cypress Island. And we saw only two people; they came roaring up to the beach in a runabout, ground the bow against the shore. One of them stood up and leaned on the windshield. He said, "Would you like a sockeye?"

We'd anchored just south of Bark Island, tucked far enough in below the bulbed point of Cypress Island to keep us out of

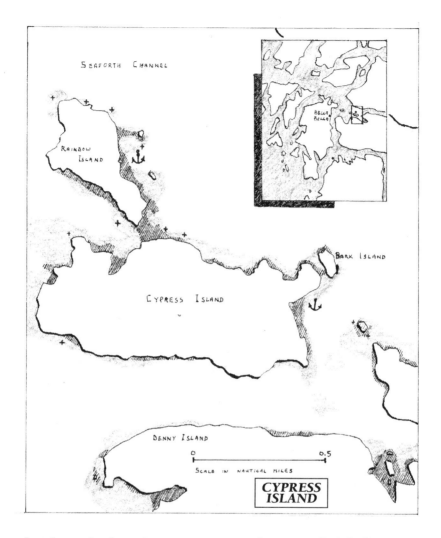

CYPRESS ISLAND

the channel where it narrows past a drying reef. A little stream trickled across our beach, past an old campsite of the Little People. We'd caught a fish that morning as we crossed the top of Raymond Channel, so we said thank you but no; we didn't need another salmon.

He looked sadly down at the floor of the boat. He had it there, wrapped in burlap for us. And with his foot, he covered it up again.

"Are you staying the night?" he said.

I said, "Yes."

"There's a better place," he said. "Just around the corner. You take your boat there, and you'll find a real beach."

But we went east instead, up into Gunboat Passage. And it was two nights before we came back across the top of Cypress Island and anchored east of Rainbow.

The wind was from the west, funnelling through the channels, and we had to snug right in toward the shore to shelter from it. The anchors seemed to cling by only the tips of their flukes to a rocky bottom, but our friend was right; it was a nicer spot.

There was an islet ahead of us, a rock to our right and another behind us, but we felt quite safe in there as long as the wind stayed from the west. On the morning low tide, we walked out on the isthmus to the islet, then south down Rainbow Island; and right across to Cypress. And then, with a change in the winds, we collected water at our first beach, and continued on our way.

Either of the beaches can be used as a fair-weather anchorage. But when the wind blows from the south or east, I'd prefer to be somewhere else. On the whole, I'd rather be in Shearwater.

≈ 14 ≈
KYNUMPT HARBOUR

chart 3720/3787

We were going north, heading for home up Seaforth Channel, when we came upon Kynumpt Harbour for the first time. It was a windy day, with whitecaps and a steep chop that burst into cold showers of spray each time we fell shuddering into a trough. I was cold and miserable, but Kristin sat smiling in the cockpit, waving to each boat as it rolled past in a spindrift cloud. Finally, we were heading home.

An hour from Dryad Point—we'd gone barely two miles—a large bay opened on the shore of Campbell Island. I saw a beach of shells backed by bushes, a quiet cove sparkling in the sun. I said, "Let's go in there."

"What?" said Kristin. "It's not even noon. We don't know what it's like in there. There might be rocks all over the place. We'll never get home, making short little trips."

I said, "We've got the chart." And she said, "Fine. Then go in. Then just go ahead in, and I hope you don't hit anything." Then she turned her back and sat scowling up the channel as we passed Active Islet and slid into Kynumpt.

The sea flattened. The wind vanished, and with it went the hiss and roar of waves. We could hear birds, feel the sun again. And Kristin looked up at the apple trees on one side, the black-berry thickets on the other—at the long strand of beach—and decided, grudgingly, that maybe it was quite a nice place after all.

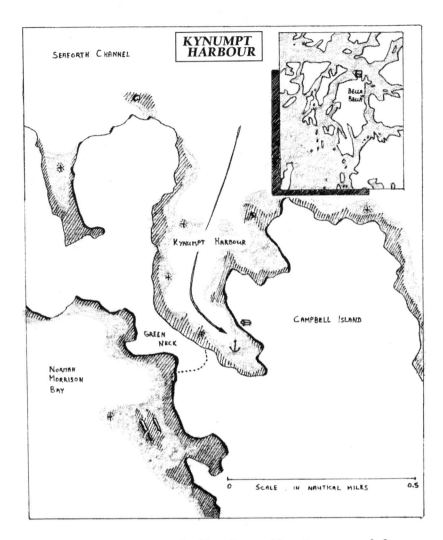

We rowed ashore, picked apples and berries, crossed the narrow isthmus of Green Neck for a walk along Norman Morison Bay. Among the beach shells, I picked up what I thought was a bit of carved argillite, though it turned out to be a bit of old battery casing. That night we listened to flights of geese whistling past, and the clang of the bell-buoy off Dall Rocks.

We saw Kynumpt at its best that day, without the flotilla of boats that often crowd the anchorage, without the masses of garbage that accumulate after infrequent picnics and rare late-night beer parties. A few years later I'd listen to the rattle of empty cans washing on the tide line, and a drunken voice bellowing at the cruising boats: "Wake up, you dog****ers! You lazy buncha dog****ers!"

Crumbling walls mark the remains of the Strom family homestead in Kynumpt Harbour.

Anchorage is good just about anywhere in the mud-bottomed harbour, though reefs extend from the south and western shores. But most boats make their way right into the elbow behind Spratt Point. It's shallow there, and sheltered, and there's room for several boats. A lot of debris lies on the bottom in the form of old cables and car tires, though, and care should be taken to ensure the anchor is really holding.

The crumbling cabin on the north shore was built by a pioneer homesteader. He is remembered in the harbour's local name: Strom Bay. Fred Strom planted the apple trees and cultivated the narrow spit of land shown on the chart as Green Neck. The first few times we anchored at Kynumpt, Kristin would stop at his grave in the cherry tree grove and leave wildflowers there. But the gravemarker has now disappeared.

Long ago Kynumpt was a summer camp for the Heiltsuk people. Berry pickers still come from Bella Bella to gather the uncommon variety of blackberries that run rampant across Green Neck. The bushes grow far higher than a man's height, and turn the trails crossing the spit to dark tunnels.

The most obvious trail begins among the cherry trees and winds through the berry patch to Norman Morison Bay on Raymond Passage. There are ruins of a boatyard among the trees on the north shore; interesting fences and pens are scattered all through the woods between the two harbours.

A creek drains into Kynumpt's inner bay, but the water is

almost stagnant and unappealing. And though the beach is often littered with garbage, Kynumpt is sometimes used by kayakers.

We sat at a small fire one evening and watched a party of them come around the point. They looked like water-boatmen, with their paddles rising and falling, skittering across a sea that turned from blue to red. They grew slowly larger as they came closer, and closer, and closer again. And with a rasp of gravel they landed right at our feet. In a moment, in a rattle of tent poles and mess kits, they'd set up camp beside us, so close our smoke wafted across them. I threw on another handful of wet bark.

"This is a nice beach," said one of them.

"Yes," said Kristin, barely looking up. "There's lots of room. In both directions."

≈ 15 ≈
MOUAT COVE

chart 3728

I wrote in the logbook: "Fog in the channel, and rising northwesterly winds lead us to a secluded anchorage just east of Ivory Island." It was Mouat Cove, well inside the entrance to Berry Inlet and 2.7 miles east of the lightstation at Ivory. Warns the *Sailing Directions*: "Berry Inlet is useless as an anchorage; however, small vessels can find shelter in Mouat Cove. Local knowledge is recommended."

We took the *Pilot*'s recommended route through the Evening Islets. And as we turned in to Mouat Cove, between the southern point and the islet opposite it, the bottom rose alarmingly on the depth sounder. But Kristin, in the bow, saw nothing. We went straight through and anchored in the middle of the cove, in a scene by the Group of Seven.

Numerous rocky islets are scattered through the bay. The largest are capped by twisted trees that sprout from a shag of bushes and lichen, crowding on the rock like shipwrecked sailors atop a raft. We rowed among them, and drifted over submerged reefs and ledges, more numerous by far than the chart seemed to indicate.

Few people come here. A little bird, tame as a budgie, landed on the dinghy and looked at me with its head cocked sideways. It perched on the jibsheet, then hopped to the cabin top and peered down through the hatch. It didn't mind us; it ignored the dog. But it turned up its nose at a soda cracker laid out for it on the deck, and flew off into the trees.

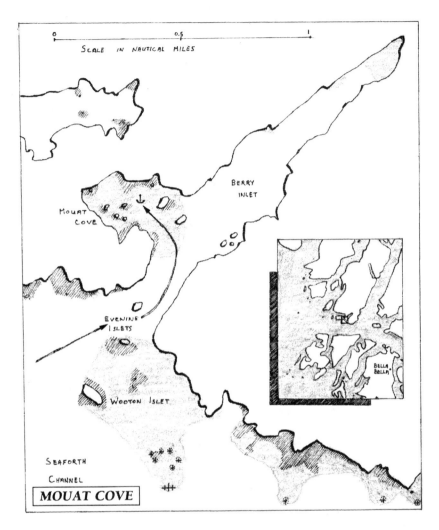

MOUAT COVE

All night and through the next morning we listened to the hoot of the Ivory Island foghorn as tendrils of mist came drifting through the trees. When the sky cleared at noon, and the noise stopped, we were off again. And we added Mouat Cove to the list of places we'd return to someday.

That day didn't come for four more years. But Mouat hadn't changed at all. I doubt it ever will. It was low tide when we anchored in the exact same spot, and the islet seemed to spread at its base like a crumbling cake. Birds we never saw made strange, eerie cries from the trees.

"Oh," said Kristin, shivering at the sound. "If a woman lost a baby, that sound would break her heart."

≈ 16 ≈
POWELL ANCHORAGE

chart 3710

Most small boats going up the Inside Passage turn north at Ivory Island and cut through Reid Passage, the route taken by Captain Vancouver's open boats. Like those sailors of two centuries ago, today's voyagers settle in at Oliver Cove and wait for the tide through Perceval Narrows.

It's a good anchorage; we sat out a forty-knot gale in Oliver Cove. We've explored the ruins of the cabins and barn, walked part way up the trail that heads off into the bush. But we've always been happy to haul the anchors out of the mud, and put poor old Lady Trutch's impenetrable passage off the beam. Oliver Cove Marine Park encompasses seventy-four hectares at the northeast end of Reid Passage, including narrow little Passage Cove at its south end. But its surrounding bays and harbours go largely unexplored.

One of the nicest spots we've ever found lies just a mile and a half to the south, at the edge of Powell Anchorage. The anchorage itself is too deep and broad for most pleasure boats, but the small bay at its western edge is a wonderful place on a quiet summer night.

The small-scale chart 3728 isn't much help here. You need the close-up view on chart 3710, "Channels East of Milbanke Sound."

The approach is simple: when heading north, swing well past Harmston Island and the Muster Rock buoy, then follow the

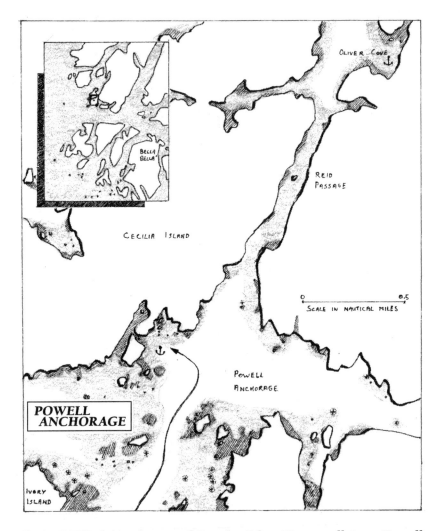

deep-water channel east of Branks Islet. Keep well into Powell Anchorage, until you've opened the gap between the bulbous peninsula on Cecilia Island and the large islet off its tip. Don't go north of the gap, as the water shoals there and is speckled with underwater rocks, but stay clear of the reef lying off the Roar Islets. Anchor in the basin between the islets and the southeast tip of Cecilia Island. Dangers are clearly visible on the large-scale chart.

We saw deer in here, on the drying flat through the gap, and a large bear plodding along the beaches to the north. On the islet fringed by drying reefs we found parts of an animal skeleton, and called the place Skull Island. In the evening of a blistering hot day it was the perfect spot for a salmon barbecue, one spot of several in the area that would be idyllic for the Little People.

Years later, travelling alone up the coast, I was surprised to see four bears on the shores of this cove. They shuffled along, back and forth, digging little crabs from the stones. I watched them from a small beach on Skull Island, shaded by tree boughs and cushioned by a band of long-leaved grass.

In the afternoon the wind changed unexpectedly to the southeast. Within hours the Ivory Island lightstation reported a three-foot sea and winds at fourteen knots. When the tide rose over the reefs ahead of the boat, leaving just a patch of land and a few jagged rocks, large logs came riding in on the low chop and swirled past in the current flowing up Blair Inlet. Behind me, little mini-breakers splashed on the rocky point.

The wind eased with the turn of the tide, and I settled in for a calm night with no worries or fears. But if the wind had really blown, I would have headed north to Oliver Cove.

≈ 17 ≈
RESCUE BAY

chart 3734/3711

Jackson Narrows is so narrow that fishing boats raise their trolling poles before passing through. Even on the close-up chart 3711, "Plans in the Vicinity of Princess Royal Island," where one inch equals 1,000 feet, the navigable channel is barely wider than the broad end of a toothpick. But it's less than half a mile from one end of the narrows to the other, and a passage through it involves only one turn to starboard, one turn to port. And many boaters rate the brief transit of Jackson Narrows high among the pleasures of a journey along the Inside Passage.

There's no reason why anyone *has* to go that way: Oscar Passage is broad and free from dangers; the route outside Cecilia and up Finlayson Channel is seven miles shorter. But every night two or three boats anchor in Rescue Bay, either after transiting the narrows or waiting for the tide to change. It's just a nice way to go.

The *Sailing Directions* is particularly cautious about this route. "Jackson Narrows (52°31′ N, 128°18′ W) near the east end of Jackson Passage is obstructed by rocks and drying reefs. The navigable passage through the narrows, suitable for small craft, is close to the Susan Island shore and should only be attempted at HW slack."

We've gone through on low-water slack, but not on a particularly low tide. It's definitely more pleasurable with an extra

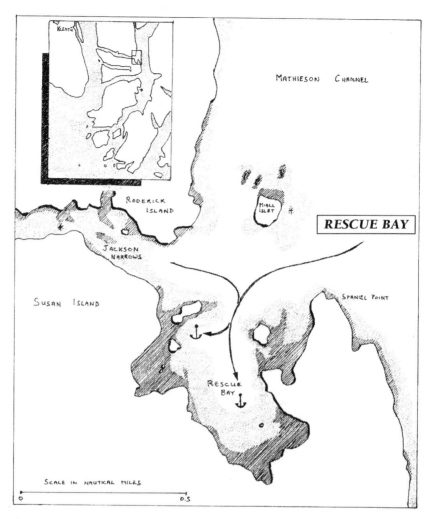

fifteen feet of water under the keel. But most fishboats just barrel through no matter what the tide is doing. And that's the only scary thing about Jackson Narrows; you never know if there's another boat coming at you from the other side.

The narrows have been preserved as a park but, unfortunately, Jackson Passage is not as attractive as it once was. There's been extensive logging on the south shore, and a fish farm may be moored in the bay on the north side. But it's still a pleasant route between Mathieson and Finlayson channels.

Jackson Narrows Marine Park includes the large bay just west of the narrows, and runs east to the edge of Rescue Bay, the traditional place to wait for slack water. Most boats anchor in the south end, where the only hazard is a single rock that dries at three feet. An attractive alternative if the bay is crowded is the nook between the two islets in the northwest corner.

The bottom drops quickly here, so care is needed when anchoring. And watch for the reef that extends east into the entrance of Rescue Bay.

I've heard wolves howling from the forest on one moon-bright night, and strange birds that made odd, bubbling sounds that had me looking constantly to see if I'd left the radio on. Gaggles of geese gather on the grassy shores in the northwest corner by the mouths of several small streams.

KLEMTU PASSAGE

Klemtu Passage is in a strategic spot. It's about midway between Jackson Narrows and Meyers Narrows, a little more than twenty miles south of Green Inlet and a good day's travel north from Kynumpt Harbour. For northbound boats, it's the last place to choose between the Inside Passage and the outer route. Heading south, you can turn east through Jackson Passage or keep going down Finlayson Channel and Milbanke Sound. When weather conditions are changeable, we often end up poring over the charts in Klemtu Passage, setting our route according to the latest forecast.

A series of small islands forms a sheltered anchorage at the south end of the passage. Clothes Bay is the most popular spot, offering good holding in sand and mud, with depths of three to five fathoms. But boats can anchor just about anywhere inside the narrow channel formed by the islands, all the way south to Fish Island. Shoal ground extends west from Star Island and east from the main shore, but careful navigators can slip easily between them. Anchoring behind the Stockade Islands, though in slightly deeper water, helps reduce the wake from passing fishboats. Few of them slow down.

There is so much boat traffic through Klemtu Passage that the beaches collect large amounts of junk and garbage. Right at the end of the sheltered inner channel, south of the shoals behind Fish

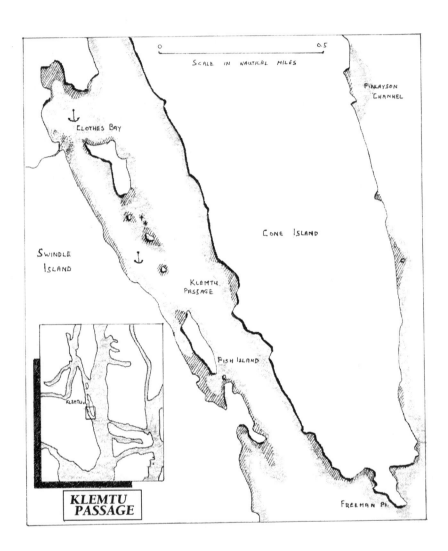

KLEMTU
PASSAGE

Drowned by a high tide, this wreck of a small fishboat lies off Klemtu Passage.

Island, the tide laps around a half-sunken fishboat and other bits of beached and rusted visions.

Klemtu, one mile north of Clothes Bay, has a fuel dock and post office. Toward the north end of the village, behind the fuel dock, a well-stocked store houses a small cafe. A boardwalk runs along the shore from one set of wharves to another. The public docks are in the middle; the dock at the south end is for float planes only.

≈ 19 ≈
JORGENSEN HARBOUR

chart 3734

Jorgensen Harbour, a mile and a half south of the eastern entrance of Meyers Passage, is the best place to wait for a favourable tide at Meyers Narrows.

The *Sailing Directions* offers alternatives immediately east and west of the narrows, but Jorgensen Harbour gets a boat off the main passage while keeping it within three miles of the narrows.

There is a shallow channel leading into the harbour around the northern shore of the unnamed island. For boats with limited ground tackle, anchorage is best just to the west of the island or close toward the tiny islet at the west side of the bay.

Meyers Narrows, shown in precise detail on chart 3710, can be passed easily at high slack. With a least depth of four feet, it's usually possible to slip through at low slack. Fishboats seem to forge through at any time; the current shouldn't exceed three knots. Masses of kelp are a big help in defining the passage, almost a straight course from end to end.

As with most places, Meyers Narrows only seems difficult the first time.

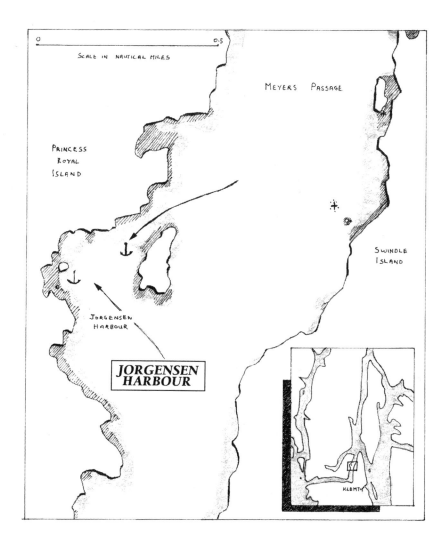

≈ 20 ≈
MONK BAY

On the chart Monk Bay is an unappealing place. The soundings are scant and of small encouragement: sixty-one fathoms at the mouth of the bay, twenty-one fathoms deep inside it. The *Sailing Directions* dismisses it with one sentence: "Monk Bay, between Dallain Point and Hague Point, is too deep for anchorage."

We came whistling down Laredo Channel in a strong northwester, not knowing what to expect at Monk Bay. *Nid* surged and rolled through the swells, the jib collapsing in the lee of the main then snapping open. We passed the shoals off Dallain Point, then dipped the rail in the water as we rounded up to tack into the bay. It opened up before us, broad and wild. And we were right inside, with three hundred feet of water still under the keel, when we lowered the sails and started the engine. In the first cove, sunlight glittered on sand and rows of bleached logs. A low swell sucked at the rocky headland, and an otter swam in broad circles across the mouth. We went straight in.

I wrote in the log: "Anchored in a beautiful bay, rock-sided with a sandy beach at the head. The sand was so fine and thick that our feet, and the dog's, sank in deeply. No fresh water."

Right at the southern entrance to Laredo Channel, this nook in Monk Bay would be perfect for kayakers and other Little People taking the other inside passage.

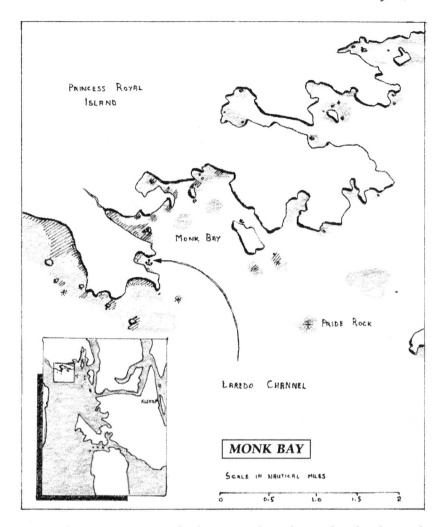

In the morning I took the water barrels in the dinghy and found a good stream one bay over. The water was clear as glass, cold as ice. In the afternoon we tried cutting across the peninsula to the beaches of Laredo Channel. But everywhere we walked were signs of bears—claw marks and scat—so we didn't go further than fifty yards.

Princess Royal seems to have a larger bear population than any of the coastal islands. We've seen several black bears on the shore, but none of the white Kermodes that roam the island.

≈ 21 ≈
SMITHERS ISLAND

Laredo Channel, a major route for deep-sea ships, lies in a direct path for southeast and northwest winds. On calm days, summer fog can linger well into the afternoon, lowering visibility to just a few yards. And the shore is irregular, sometimes steep and rock-bound. So when you start looking for a spot sheltered from the wind and well out of the channel, your choices are quickly limited.

The eastern shore, Princess Royal Island, is indented by four deep inlets. All are entered through narrow passages where the tide runs strongly. At Kent Inlet and Commando Inlet, the stream can reach eight or ten knots.

But at Helmcken Inlet, midway through the four, an island divides the entrance in two. And a little bay on the island offers confined but secure anchorage.

Says the *Sailing Directions*: "Anchorage and shelter for small craft can be obtained in a small bight in the south shore of Smithers Island, in 8 fathoms (15 metres)."

A large rock lies east of the island, and should be passed well to the south; the passage between the rock and the island is choked with rock and kelp. But otherwise the entrance is clear.

The depth drops to more than a hundred feet beyond a bar that lies across the entrance, and the bight is narrow and quite confined. It's a weirdly sheltered place, just deep enough to keep

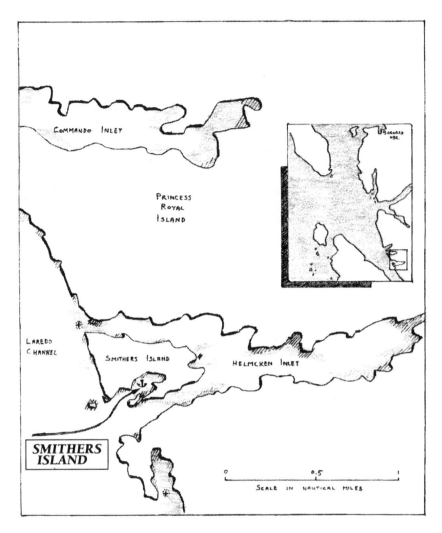

Inside the map:

COMMANDO INLET

PRINCESS
ROYAL
ISLAND

BARNARD
HBR.

LAREDO
CHANNEL

SMITHERS ISLAND

HELMCKEN INLET

**SMITHERS
ISLAND**

0   0.5   1

SCALE IN NAUTICAL MILES

a boat out of northerly winds in the channel, but still open to
gusts that can swirl in from any direction. There can be heavy
surf on the off-lying rock, but only a gentle swell inside the bay.

Seals live here and otters, on the high, moss-covered islets
that form the best anchorage within the bight. The shore drops
straight to the water in sheer cliffs crowded with a fascinating
zoo of underwater animals. There are even turban snails; their
elegant, swirling shells can be picked off the ground among the
island's rocks.

We anchored here at sunset one day in August. I took the
dog to the islet and let her run off her day's energy, hunting otters
through the drying clefts in the rock. When we rowed back to

A stern line holds Nid *in place in a little bay on Smithers Island.*

the boat, in the last of the twilight, a big black bear came lumbering out of the bush on Smithers Island and swam across to the islet.

"I didn't know bears would swim like that," said Kristin, watching from the companionway.

"No," I said. So much for our theory that tiny islets are free of bears.

EMILY CARR INLET

chart 3719/3724/3737

For day after day we motored north through flat seas and driving rain. We crossed the mouth of Surf Inlet on a cold and miserable day, and kept on going up the narrow gap to Doig Anchorage. And there, at the edge of Emily Carr Inlet, we found something to cheer us from the weather.

Someone picked a wonderful place to name after British Columbia's best-known artist. The surf breaks on offshore islands fringed by sandy beaches. Ravens and eagles perch in tall, ancient cedars. Wolves and deer and bears roam through the forests.

It's a place where you can walk over thick carpets of lichen and moss. It's a place where you can find signs of ancient logging, when the only tools were stone-head axes and fires brewed in hollowed trunks. It's a place that, once you've seen it, you'll never forget.

In Doig Anchorage we tied up to a logboom across a creek mouth. We tied cannonballs to the bow and stern lines and heaved them over the logs. The weight kept us nestled up to the boom, and other cannonballs tied to the fenders kept us bumpered off them. We filled our water barrels, then watched ravens picking through the shoals, collecting clams from the mud. We spent a whole day rowing among the islands of Emily Carr, then left the next dawn with tendrils of fog drifting through the trees.

The next year we found a portable camp tied to the boom.

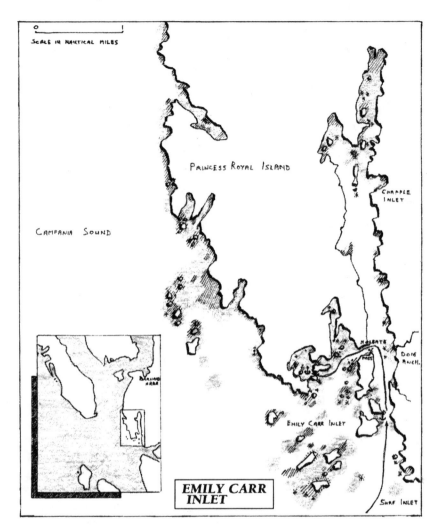

EMILY CARR
INLET

But we collected water from a long hose that snaked down from the cliffs, then anchored off a fine beach that joined two islands, the sand pockmarked by deer and wolf tracks. On a high tide we took the boat into the broad lagoon on the inlet's west side and anchored in a spot where it seemed that no one had ever been before.

The point dividing Emily Carr Inlet from Chapple Inlet has been logged. Bare slopes gleam like scar tissue as you approach the inlet from the south. Plans call for much more extensive logging in the area, particularly in the hills to the northwest, along a system of roads that will all lead to Kiln Bay. But for now, Emily Carr Inlet is a paradise for boaters and kayakers.

There are many reefs and rocks within the inlet, and on days

Ancient forests flourish on the islands at the mouth of Chapple Inlet. The large cedar on the left has been culturally modified; a strip of bark was cut from the trunk long ago.

of westerly wind, the swell can be heavy. But the dangers are shown clearly on chart 3737, and boats with local knowledge troll right among the rocks.

Some points worth knowing:

~ The *Sailing Directions* says Holgate Passage is obstructed at its east end by a drying reef connecting to Webber Island. At low tide, the passage is extremely narrow but quite visible. At high tide, it can be negotiated safely by positioning someone on the bow as you keep toward the logged-off shore.

~ A rock lies in the middle of the entrance into the westward lagoon. We anchored off the entrance until the tide was high, then went straight down the middle. We came out at mid-tide and banged the keel on the hidden rock. *Nid* draws about four and a half feet—give or take a little nick.

~ A nice beach joins the first two islands you pass on the

way up into Chapple Inlet. There are always deer tracks in the thick, coarse sand—sometimes wolf and bear. Though the cove to the east dries most of the way out, it's possible to anchor just off the main channel into the anchorage. Tidal currents can be quite strong, and the room for a boat to swing with ebb and flood is limited by shoals at the north side of the cove. A prominent boulder sits on this reef; coming in at half tide, I thought it was a dome-tent floating there.

~ When the ebb tide from Surf Inlet opposes a westerly wind, a very heavy swell can build up off the entrance. Twenty-four hours after a period of westerly winds to thirty knots, we found swells five to six feet high rolling over the bar extending northwest from Wearmouth Rock.

≈ 23 ≈
GREEN INLET

chart 3738

Sixteen miles north of Boat Bluff, Green Inlet is one of the regular stops on the marine highway. There are tidal falls at its head, and a huge lagoon almost the size of the inlet, but most cruisers never get that far. Horsefly Cove, less than a mile from the mouth, is as deep into Green Inlet as just about anybody goes.

There are shallow spots off the little inlet forming the cove, but otherwise the anchorage is free of dangers. It's deep—thirteen fathoms just a few feet from shore—and sometimes quite crowded. Old rope ends droop from several trees; it seems to be standard procedure to lie with a line to shore.

We stopped here for the first time in 1989, collected water at the stream in the northwest corner, walked the dog on the spit separating the mainland from the island. Masses of multi-legged sunstars had stranded themselves in the rocky tidepools. They slid back and forth like Ouija shuttles through the shallow ponds. And all over the rock lay severed arms and legs, as though some horrible starfish massacre had happened there.

Though the anchorage has been named a marine park, a logboom and floathouse had appeared in Horsefly Cove by the summer of 1994. It stretched across the mouth of the creek, taking up a good chunk of the bay and the shallowest part of the anchorage. In the evening, a tugboat came in and tied to a barge at the boom. Then a lightplant started up, horribly loud, and roared far into the night.

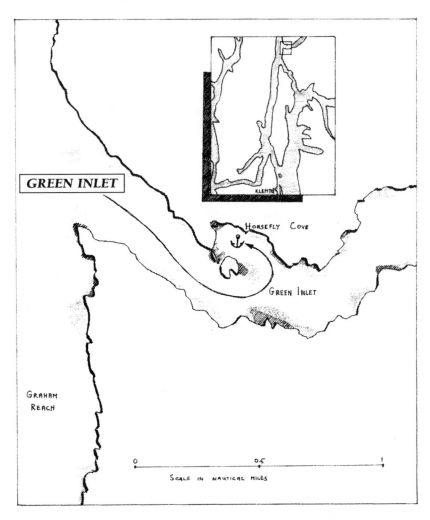

Green Inlet Marine Park includes all of Horsefly Cove and its small islets, as well as a good chunk of the mainland shore behind it. Bring lots of anchor chain, and a fly swatter.

≈ 24 ≈
BUTEDALE

chart 3739

When we first stopped at Butedale, in the summer of 1989, it was like calling at a ghost town. We pushed open sagging doors, passed through empty rooms and abandoned homes. We walked through the net loft with our boots banging like clock springs, ducked under strands of dusty webbing. Down a crumbling staircase we went and, in the electrician's room, saw his motors and machines still spread out on the workbench. In the office we found masses of papers spilling from shelved walls. In the home behind it bags of clothes and children's toys covered the floor, as though the people were just moving out, or the ghosts were just moving in.

Year by year, every time we saw it, Butedale had changed a bit, declined a little more. Buildings tumbled and huge sections of wharf collapsed into the bay. Someone chopped down the power poles; someone burned the largest house right to its foundations. And then, in the summer of 1994, I turned into the bay and saw fresh paint shining on the walls of the store and office. New planks were laid into the boardwalk; baskets of flowers bloomed on the dock. On the point below the burned foundations, the grass was cut and exotic trees were blooming again. Always a picturesque place, Butedale looked brand new in places, while other buildings still leaned like drunks, their windows glassless, their roofs and eaves drawn with squiggle lines. It was as though someone had propped up a grime-smeared painting, an old master, and started retouching it at random.

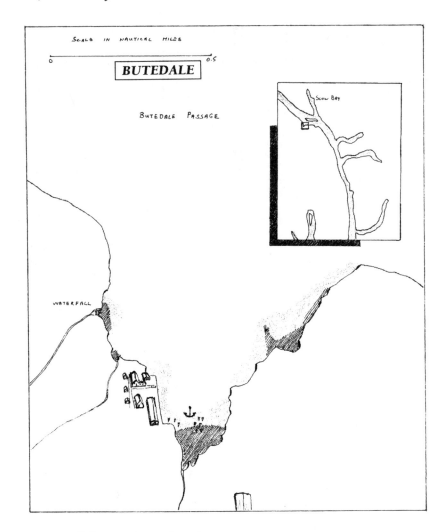

Butedale was in its Renaissance.

Earlier that year, after nearly ten years of sitting abandoned and neglected, the octogenarian cannery-village was purchased by the Butedale Founders Association, a group of U.S. and Canadian families. Drawing on their own expertise as house builders, brick masons, restauranteurs and bookkeepers, the Founders are bringing Butedale back into service.

As of this writing, plans are to have a fuel barge in the bay by the summer of 1995. Facilities will re-open for showers and laundry; a store will sell ice cream and snacks. Future plans include providing ice for commercial fishboats, setting up a gift shop and small grocery store. And eventually, the Founders hope to outfit

Old pilings held structures of the Chinese village in the cannery's hey-day.

canoe trips on the huge expanse of Butedale Lake, to serve as a base for freshwater and saltwater fishing, and to cater to kayakers exploring the Inside Passage. Also for the first time in a decade, boats will be charged a modest moorage at the old cannery docks. But anchorage will still be free throughout the bay. And it seems that most boaters will welcome the change.

I anchored at the back of the bay, where the water was still a hundred feet deep, the stern nestled among the pilings of the long-gone Chinese village. Two of the Founders were getting an early start on their work in that summer of 1994. Builder Mark Erickson and his partner Steve McGrath had divided a Herculean list of labours. Erickson had just finished clearing the brush from a grove of exotic tress and had his tools spread through the lobby of the Butedale Hotel. McGrath was on a ladder adding the last bit of paint to a reborn office when a huge motoryacht came gliding into the bay.

It was a modern yacht, with banks of darkened windows and high-powered skiffs hoisted to the aft deck. It stopped below the old wharf, water burbling from the exhaust, and sat there, its band of windows like sunglasses perched on a huge, white nose. No one came on deck. A loudhailer crackled, then spoke.

McGrath waved down from his ladder. In a tiny voice I could hardly hear, he outlined his plans: gas and diesel in '95, full service the year after. Then the boat answered, in a southern accent, blasting electronically back from the hills. It sounded—engines throbbing and water burbling—like the Wizard of Oz: a great and powerful thing with a little man inside.

"Well, that's great news," it said. "Great news. We'll be sure to stop next year. Come and see you."

Then it backed into the bay and water frothed at the stern as it turned in place and headed out again on its way.

Butedale is one of the most scenic spots on the coast. It sits in a high-sided valley beside a tumbling waterfall. The buildings are brown and grey, tinted with rust and moss green, all earth colours, as though the village grew complete from the land. I walked with McGrath up to the top of the falls, on to the lake along a game trail in the woods, then back down the long boardwalk.

He felt lucky to be there. Like the other Founders, McGrath was bringing his whole family to Butedale. He was becoming a Canadian citizen; he was practising his vowels.

"From 1908 to 1967, this was a summer town of four hundred people," he said. "Now it's a ghost town. And I feel privileged to be a part of that history."

We passed a row of fresh-painted houses, the old hotel with its rotunda full of wood-working tools. "It's not going to die anymore," he said. "The buildings aren't going to fall down. It's pretty exciting to know we're going to make a difference up here."

I rowed to the foot of the waterfall and drifted in the spray and foam, held there by its current, then crossed the bay back to little *Nid*.

That night was dark and overcast. I sat up for a long time staring at the old buildings on the shore. It was eerie seeing a light burning among them, a single window spilling out a yellow glow. The last time we'd anchored here, Kristin had stayed on the boat while I went prowling through the cannery. She was saddened by the ruins and said: "If I wanted to see squalor I could stay at home."

I walked alone through the store and office, through the hotel, and eventually climbed up to the net loft with its weird spider webs of nylon. There were square holes in the floor, beams above them for hoisting nets, and they looked like empty gallows with traps swung open. And as I stood up there I heard footsteps below me.

Someone was walking on the lower floor, boots clumping on the planks. I peered down through a swirl of dust, but there was nobody there. And when I looked out through a doorway, I could see *Nid* out in the bay, all alone, Kristin poking head and shoulders through the hatch.

Probably the wind in the tin roofing; that's what it was. Just the wind.

≈ 25 ≈
KLEKANE INLET

chart 3739

Even two centuries later you feel sorry for Captain George Vancouver when you read his journals of the trip north of Princess Royal Island. He must have known by then that he'd never find a Northwest Passage, must have dreaded sending his boats up each narrow, steep-sided inlet. He would have longed for Hawaii again as the north-coast rains came pouring down, week after week. By day he could barely make progress in his ungainly converted coal carrier; by night he couldn't even find a spot to anchor it. Fraser Reach and Graham Reach are both abysmally deep: in centre channel even the shallow places are a thousand feet down. Almost the entire shoreline of Princess Royal Island is rocky and steep, and the mainland shore isn't much better. Vancouver soon learned to nudge the *Discovery* against the shore and spend the night tied to trees, with the ship's side against the rocks.

"Our present resting place was perfectly safe," he wrote, "but this is not the case against every part of these rocky precipices, as they are frequently found to jut out a few yards, or a little beneath low water mark; and if a vessel should ground on any of those projecting parts about high water, she would, on the falling tide, if heeling from the shore, be in a very dangerous situation."

A series of inlets poke like fingers into the mainland shore, but for the most part they're just minor versions of the major

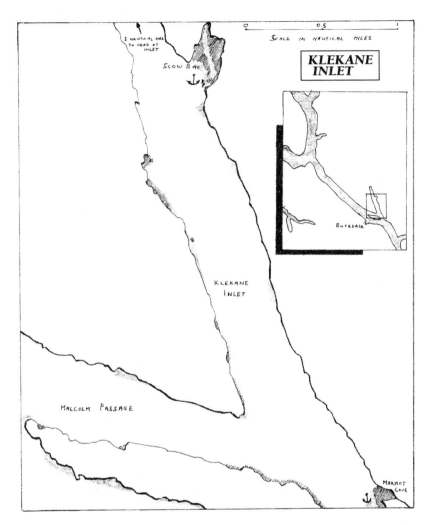

channels—deep, dark, and gloomy in the rain.

But here or there the chart will show a splash of green in an inlet cove, a dot of blue marking shallows big enough for *Nid*, if not for Vancouver's hundred-foot *Discovery*. So when we saw Scow Bay on the Butedale chart, we decided we'd go in there instead of anchoring off the old cannery again, and we turned north at Work Island and up the inlet called Klekane.

From the entrance it was three miles to Scow Bay on Klekane's eastern shore. The chart showed a stream winding over drying flats, a row of dolphins that would take a stern line. "I'll bet nobody goes there," I said as we crawled up the inlet at three knots with the little diesel whining and shaking under the cockpit, the staysail just filling in a light breeze. But we were only halfway from the entrance when a boat appeared around the point behind us.

It came climbing up out of the water, a little catboat with an orange tarp wrapped over the furled sail. Water churned white at its bow.

"He'll be going right to Scow Bay," I said.

"I doubt it," said Kristin. "It's a big inlet."

I gave the throttle a nudge; the boat quivered and shook. Behind us, the catboat kept gaining. He crept up on our starboard side; I steered closer and closer to the shore. Soon we could see a face in the cockpit, bearded and dour. We could hear the water rippling at his bow.

"A classic stern chase," I said.

"Huh?" said Kristin.

With half a mile to go, I took down the staysail. With a quarter mile to go, he was only a boat-length behind us. And just yards from the bay, he forced through between us and the shore, our boats rocking in each other's wake, the rocks flashing past a few feet from his rail. He didn't wave; he didn't even smile. But then, neither did we. In the logbook, I called him "a surly, brutish fellow."

He didn't stop at the dolphins, but kept going across the mouth of the little bay. Side by side, in silence, we anchored. I took a line to the pilings; he took a little stern anchor to the mudflats. We never said a word to each other.

I thought we'd got the better spot, until we looked at the cliffs beside us, a nearly vertical rise to twenty-seven hundred feet, and saw the avalanche tracks sweeping down. On the little beach at the bottom, huge boulders lay in a heap, like cars stacked at an auto wrecker's.

"Oh," said Kristin. "We could get squashed here."

At low tide, the bay dried to a flat of mud and grass that reached out nearly to the dolphins. We found the ruins of what we thought had been a cannery; a great iron ring rusted in the mud. Bear tracks wound through the freshly dried grass. Along the cliffs, underground streams roared and gurgled through the jumbled rocks, spewing seawater somehow, icy cold.

During the night a small powerboat anchored close ahead of us, and we all spent the night in a little knot under the dark, brooding mountain. At dawn a white swan joined us and paddled round and round the boat.

There isn't much room for anchorage at Scow Bay. It drops off from the tidal flat to more than forty fathoms in just a few

A row of dolphins in Marmot Cove is one of the last signs of a vanishing little community.

boat lengths. The easiest spot is up against the dolphins. The safest place might be a bit further from the cliffs.

But there's another scenic spot, a different sort of anchorage, right at the mouth of Klekane Inlet.

Marmot Cove, also on the eastern shore, was once a satellite of a bustling Butedale. Like most early European settlements on the north coast, it was built on top of a much older homestead, one already developed and abandoned by Natives. Today you can still see the shell middens in the gap behind Marmot Island and, atop them like gravemarkers, the sad, mouldering ruins of the fishermen's homes. Inside Marmot Island a row of old pilings shows where the dock once stood. Now the pilings wear necklaces of old, slime-covered rope: the left-behind shorelines of people who have anchored here.

I was always intrigued by the cove when we passed, with its arc of beach coloured gold by seaweed, the sweep of brighter green behind that; it looked to me like a rainbow lying on its side and propped up against the mountains. And finally, in the late summer of 1994, I turned the boat into the cove and watched the lights swing quickly up the depth-sounder dial.

A few yards off the beach the channel is two hundred feet deep. It rises quickly to a six-fathom ledge, and I dropped the anchor there on a falling tide, snubbed the boat to a stop maybe eighty feet from the tip of Marmot Island. I tossed a stern line in the dinghy and struck out for shore. It was a sort of backwards way to do it; the tide, on both flood and ebb, flows into the cove from the south. When the drying flats behind Marmot Island are submerged, the narrow gap becomes a raceway for the flood tide. So I went one way, and *Nid* went the other.

I had to row back for a second length of rope, bend it on, and even when I had all three hundred feet stretched out, the boat was still five feet away. The dog peered down, whining and wagging her tail. I rowed and rowed, the boats swung together. Then I lunged across the gap, and barely hooked my fingertips over the toerail. I hung there, feet in one boat and hands on the other, rigid above the water like a silent-movie comic. And the dog gave a happy little yelp, and came running down to lick my fingers.

It took me an hour to get everything settled, a second anchor out where the first one should have been. And then the *Queen of the North* came barrelling round the corner, heading up Malcolm Passage, and rolled little *Nid* from rail to rail.

In the afternoon the wind came rushing up Graham Reach. It rose through the evening and into the night, when heat lightning flashed in yellowish bursts behind the mountain peaks. But Marmot Cove was sheltered from that, until the tide flooded the gap behind the island, and waves came rolling all the way from Sarah Island, twenty miles away. It was the noise that woke me at 3:00 A.M., the squeal of wooden blocks as the boom swung back and forth, the splash of water on the bow, the flap of a loosely-tied awning. But there was no danger or alarm; I was as safe there as anywhere.

A crab boat sometimes sets traps off Marmot Cove. And the Little People have stayed on the shores of the channel inside the island. It's a not a bad anchorage, if you watch the tide and weather. And not far away, in the next cove to the south, Captain Vancouver finally did find a spot to anchor his ship "with a hawser to the shore."

He stayed there a week.

≈ 26 ≈
ECLIPSE BAY

chart 3724/3737

The narrow bay poking into the bottom end of Campania Island has no official name. But Eclipse Point forms the south side of the entrance, and so I've let that serve for both purposes.

There is a campsite at the head of the bay, beside a boggy creek with a trickle of water. The bugs are bad, and the steep, wooded slopes on either side are dark and confining.

But we have a soft spot for Eclipse Bay.

Off Banks Island one year, our auxiliary diesel refused to start. The head gasket was broken, letting water into the single cylinder, and we started sailing south to the shipyard at Shearwater. We came down the outside of Campania in a light northwesterly, planning to tack up to Eclipse Bay for the night. We thought the wind, forecasted to rise, would blow us right out of the bay in the morning, and south down Laredo Channel.

But off Alexander Island the wind vanished. And I got in the dinghy, and I rowed.

It took two hours to tow the boat the mile to Eclipse Point. The sky darkened, and a swath of green light, like a pale rainbow, arched above the trees. Each sweep of the little oars churned up balloons of bright light. Kristin, in the cockpit, steered by the flicker of stars through the trees. And exactly at midnight, we dropped the anchor in Eclipse Bay in a huge flash of bioluminescent green.

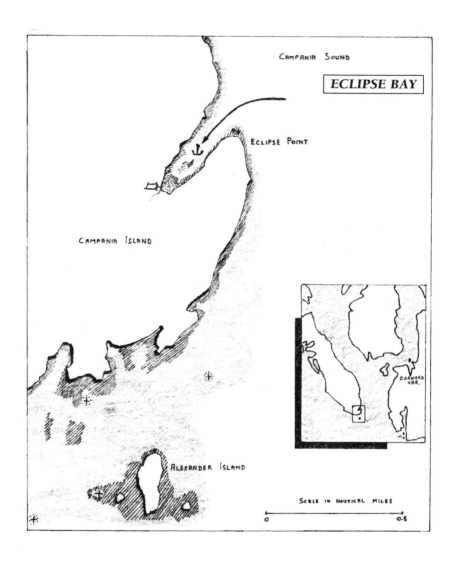

CAMPANIA SOUND

ECLIPSE BAY

ECLIPSE POINT

CAMPANIA ISLAND

BARNARD HBR.

ALEXANDER ISLAND

SCALE IN NAUTICAL MILES

0   0.5

Of course, in the morning the wind had shifted to the east, and we got out the oars again.

The log for that day says: "Tried to row out of the bay into a light breeze blowing directly toward us. Managed to get the anchor back down before we lost too much ground."

Seven miles northwest of Chapple Inlet and ten miles southeast of Barnard Harbour, little Eclipse Bay is a good spot for boats waiting for favourable conditions in the outer passages of Laredo Channel and Estevan Sound. It's well sheltered from most winds, but particularly from strong summer westerlies.

There is a Little People's spot at the back of the bay, a good campsite sheltered by trees. Nearby a small creek dribbles over grass and stones.

SQUALLY CHANNEL

chart 3742

The forecast was for northwest winds when I came out of Barnard Harbour on a foggy morning. After two nights there I was tired of having boats all around me and thought I'd cross to Fish Bay, just five miles away at the bottom of Gil Island.

In Squally Channel the fog still lay in thick dollops—great, boiling masses of it bubbled like porridge over Ashdown Island—but I didn't worry about it; I wasn't going that far. I crossed through thin, wispy bands and homed in—like a moth—on the light at York Point. And I followed the shore west toward Fish Bay.

It would have been a nice, easy trip if the fog hadn't suddenly closed in around me, if the wind hadn't picked up with awful suddenness, from the south, and brought those high banks of fog tumbling toward me like avalanche snow. But I couldn't go back, so I moved in toward the shore until the trees loomed like skeletons through the mist, and kept on going.

Waves were breaking off the mouth of Fish Bay. They piled up against the rocks and burst on the shore, and row after row of them went marching straight into the bay. I could see a boat in there, a grey shadow tugging wildly at its anchor. And I turned the other way, headed out into the fog and those rows of waves.

Somewhere ahead was Fawcett Point, dangling down from Gil Island, thrusting half a mile into Whale Channel like a claw scratching at the rocks that lie off its tip. I set the little staysail,

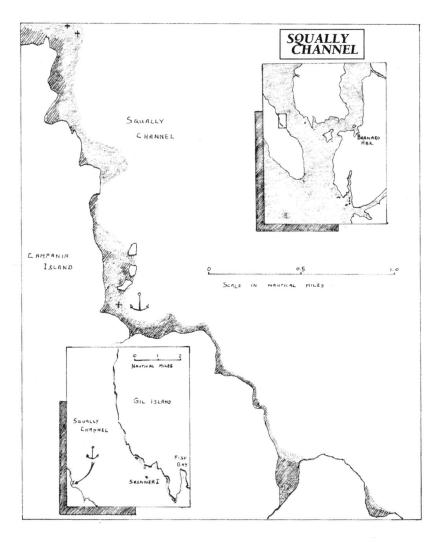

felt it strain against the sheet as the boat heeled and flounced out to sea. And the land loomed off the bow, rushing sideways in the fog as the tide carried me west. I tightened the sheet, and dollops of spray pattered on the sail. The land appeared and disappeared, circled furtively behind me. And as the rocks slid by, slick and darkly wet, I peered anxiously ahead, afraid I was only rounding the point and not the off-lying rocks.

Then I was out in Squally Channel on a grey, whitecapped sea, and the sky opened above me in a flash of blue and sun. I started looking for our anchorage ahead—our old one—the one we always think of as the place we had whales for dinner.

We'd found it then, a few years before, on another day of

unexpected southeasters. Rather than sail on through a clouded-dark and windy night, we'd turned toward the east shore of Campania Island, to the one bay that looked promising on the chart. And we'd anchored in a sandy cove, below an island where the rocks were sharp and jagged as shards of broken glass.

We built a fire in amongst them, balanced like fakirs with our dinner plates on our laps. At sunset a red sky bled down into the sea, and two grey whales came swimming past our island. They swam side by side, rising together and falling together, breathing with one loud, metallic blast, so close to each other they might have been touching flukes and fins. They passed very close, and then the two tails rose and spread, and the whales vanished into that blood-stained sea.

"Wow," said Kristin.

The place is hard to find in the confusing landscape of eastern Campania. It sits below the northern arm of a horseshoe bend of mountains, almost due west of Skinner Island. To be safe, locate the bay first at 53°5.5′ N, 129°23.5′ W. It's easiest, when approaching the shore, to pick out the large stream that comes down through a valley half a mile to the south. And the cove is not quite as smooth sided, nor as uniformly deep as the chart indicates. (We've found similar conditions at several places on chart 3742; it covers such a huge area that minor details like rocks and reefs just don't always show up.)

A small stream emerges at the southeast corner, and a large reef extends from there into the bay. Above that three small islets stretch in a line from southeast to northwest, almost connecting at very low tides. A boat can work in behind them, from the south, but the shoreline is irregular and the channel is quite shallow; I found depths of just ten feet on a seven-foot tide. Another shallow spot, and a rock, lie southwest of the islands, marked normally by fringes of kelp. The best anchorage is east of there, southeast of the first islet.

Our first morning there we woke to gusts coming over the island. Clouds raced by, below the mountain peaks but above the bay, and a swell rolled in round the point. And when we got a crackling, static-filled forecast for southeast gales, we took one look at all the open water to the east and weighed anchor for a more sheltered spot at the north end of Campania.

But when I came in alone from the fog, the wind was already easing, the sky clearing, and the forecast called for northwest winds. A whale came by that night, low and sleek, heading south. And I spent the next day exploring the beaches, the islets mazed by otter runs, the fringe of wood that stands between the shore and the open,

The east side of Campania Island is rugged and exposed. We balanced on these rocks to cook barbecued salmon over an open fire.

rocky hills of Campania Island. I watched the sun set, and listened to a distant sound, like static, as waves broke on Gil Island.

Then, out of nowhere, came a lightning storm. It woke me near midnight, the boat plunging in a heavy swell. The moon was almost full, shining through banks of scudding cloud, flickering on the wave tops. I could see the surf bursting in silver sheets behind me, hear it crashing on the islet's splintered rock.

And every minute or two the sky to the south flickered with silent lightning, a yellow glow that flashed on endless waves. I paddled out in the dinghy, headed off in the darkness feeling lonely as an astronaut loose from his spaceship. And rolled and tossed by the waves, I reset the stern anchor off the bow, lowered forty pounds of lead on the rode. And when the boat swung round and settled between both anchors, I switched on the radio and listened to the lightstation reports. Each one south of Campania noted "lightning past hour" or "distant lightning north", and I could track the progress of the little storm, imagine it sliding over Ivory Island and out past McInnes, heading safely west forty miles away. I could picture the lightkeepers peering through rain-splattered windows, their faces flashing pale in the lightning glow.

≈ 28 ≈
BARNARD HARBOUR

chart 3724/3723

Sports fishermen home in on Barnard Harbour like bees to a hive. Each evening they come buzzing in through the entrance, swarm to the head of the bay and off to the side, then settle down for the night in neat, tidy rows. But despite the apparent confusion, there's a pattern in their movement.

The harbour is a popular spot with Kitimat boaters; everyone seems to know everyone else. They come in from a day's fishing, drop their crab traps in the deep water at the east side of Cameron Cove, then anchor in the shallows on the west side. The first boats in get the best place, just inside the bay, off a curving beach and a small islet. And they space themselves from there, each little boat with a huge landing net propped upright by the cabin, as though the cove plays host nightly to a group of butterfly collectors.

We put ourselves further up the inlet, just beyond the island at Cameron Cove's south end, and remained as alone there as a foreign drone. But this is where the cruising boats anchor—off the edge of the flats with a view straight up the mountain valley—and on our second night we found ourselves ringed in by big boats with thundering engines.

Despite the vastness of Barnard Harbour, there aren't many other places to anchor. North of Cameron Cove, depths are generally greater than twenty fathoms and the shoreline is steep. The only

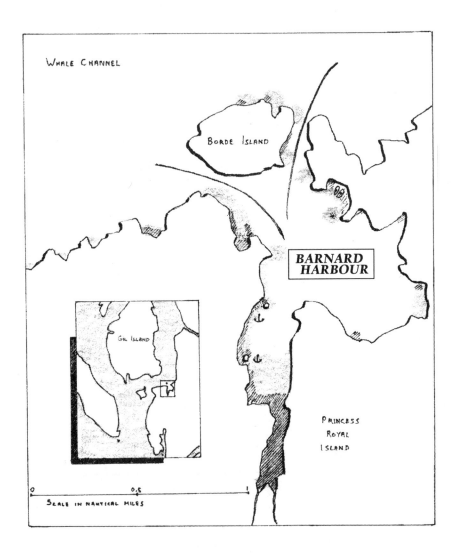

Two Rivers *and* Renner Pass *lie beached in a bay near the entrance to Barnard Harbour.*

real anchorage in the main harbour—a shallow corner to the southeast by the mouth of a creek—is filled by a floating fishing lodge. The deep cove north of there is a booming ground for a log-salvage crew, and the next little bight going north is a sort of wrecking yard. Two old work boats, the *Renner Pass* and *Two Rivers*, lie at the edge of the tide, their decks dangerously slick with weed and slime.

Summer fog often settles over the harbour and surrounding waters, and winds can pipe down through the valley to the south. But the fishing is excellent in Whale Channel and Casanave Passage. Boats frequently troll out of the harbour in the mornings, catching their first salmon before they've passed through the twin entrances east and west of Borde Island.

Large and popular, and sometimes crowded, Barnard Harbour is obviously the best anchorage in the area.

≈ 29 ≈
McMICKING INLET

For almost a week the wind had blown steadily from the northwest. It had blown without rest, through day and night, howling down Principe Channel. We'd seen huge, black-bellied clouds streaming past, like fleets of airships, Hindenburgs ripping themselves to shreds in the trees above us.

We sailed south on big, breaking waves with the mainsail double reefed, tacking down the wind as we worked our way toward McMicking Inlet. From miles away we could see Jewsbury Peninsula silhouetted against the shore of Campania Island. A little closer and we saw the surf breaking on outlying rocks, the waves piling up on the shallows there.

Once before we'd gone right by in a thirty-knot wind rather than turn onto that lee shore. We'd sailed along with fifty porpoises leaping and plunging in the waves around us, then turned north again, inside Campania, and made a huge circle of almost a hundred miles to approach the inlet again from the north on a calmer day.

But this time we went right in. We rose on the wave crests and slid, wallowing, into the troughs. Lines of surf stretched before us, then vanished behind a wall of water. Matted rafts of kelp rushed by on each side, and we surged forward, aiming for the deep-water gap south of the islets and north of the spot where the sea boiled over Logan Rock.

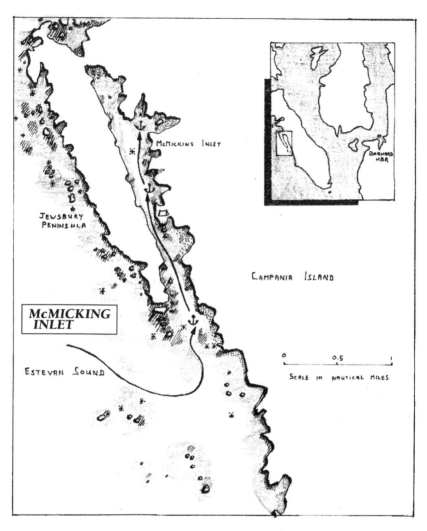

We tightened the sheets and put the waves on our beam, and water spurted up through the scuppers, poured over the foredeck. And when we passed the islets, and rounded up inside the inlet, the wind was as strong there as it was on the outside. We motored up through the first narrows and anchored above the string of beaches, in a little cove where a steel-blue chop rolled down from the head of McMicking.

"Well, we made it," I said.

"Yes. Thank God," said Kristin.

I said, "Aren't you glad to be here?"

"Oh, *being* here's okay." She made an awful face; I hoped the wind wouldn't change right then. "It's the coming in I always hate."

Deep inside McMicking Inlet, the landscape is rocky and barren.

There are LOTS of rocks in and around the entrance to McMicking Inlet, speckled over shallows that extend more than a mile from shore. In strong winds, it's uncomfortable and sometimes dangerous. But on a calm day, with careful navigation, the inlet can be approached quite easily from west through to south.

Using the islets south of the peninsula as a guide, we had no trouble picking out the channel through the reefs and kelp the first time we entered the inlet. We anchored off the largest of the pocket beaches below the nearly vertical cliffs of Mount Pender.

There were still kayak skid marks high on the sand, the first signs of the Little People that we'd had for several days. A small creek trickled down through the rocks, and we scooped water from it to fill the dinghy for a make-shift laundry tub.

This is the most scenic spot in the inlet, with a view south to an empty horizon. An immense boulder just north of the beaches offers some shelter from light winds. We've anchored on either side of it, depending on conditions, held firmly in thick sand.

But when the wind blows, we head up into the inlet.

There are two sets of narrows. The first one is obvious only at low tides, but a rocky ledge extends west from Campania almost to the peninsula. There is usually some kelp sprouting from the ledge, but not enough to safely define the passage.

Beyond it, on the east side, is a small cove that dries nearly halfway out on very low tides. On its north shore, in the crook of a small peninsula, we found one of the Little People's campsites. It had a private beach, a tent-sized clearing in the trees, and we built a fire there to barbecue salmon. In the evening we were joined by frogs that squatted at our feet like fat little Buddhas. They stared at us with huge eyes, their throats ballooning, then wandered off, one by one, into the woods.

The second narrows follows the peninsula shore; it is quite deep and free of dangers, and forms a boundary between two very different areas.

At its south end, McMicking Inlet is a lot like the northwest tip of Calvert Island. The tide rises quickly up shelves of sand; there are seagulls and cormorants everywhere. Behind the trees are vast, rolling hills of rock worn smooth by glaciers. It's a moonscape where a hiker can travel quickly inland, and climb right up the shoulder of Mount Pender to its 2,400-foot summit.

But north of the second narrows, the inlet opens into a series of coves with steep, jumbled shores. And behind those the barren boulder slopes are replaced by high, bush-covered tors and forests of ancient pines with bark like lizard scales. We anchored in the deepest cove, below an island that joined with the shore at low tide, and in the space of an afternoon saw:

~ eagles dining on a pink, shredded carcass

~ ravens lurking by them like dark shadows, obvious masters in a battle of wits

~ seals and huge fat loons

~ sandhill cranes that flew everywhere in pairs, wingtip to wingtip like honeymoon couples

~ the walls of stone fish traps on the shore beside us and across the small creek on our cove's northern shore

~ jellyfish as huge and pulpy as drowned corpses, others like drifting saucers, so many we couldn't row to shore without stirring scores of them into swirls and spirals

We rowed to the head of the inlet, walked across the isthmus to Betteridge Inlet. At night we listened to wolves calling back and forth from the hills of Campania. And in the daylight we followed their winding trails up a stream and into the barrens.

There are tiny lakes up there, muskeg and stunted trees. There are huckleberry bushes just three inches high, with fruit like trading beads. On the lakes float lily pads and by the shores stand delicate plants that catch bugs in the tongues of toothed leaves. We climbed up, like giants in this world of stunted, miniature plants, and found every summit an eagle's dinner table, the ground strewn with shells of abalone and cockle and moonsnail, each one broken open and pierced by a square hole.

And even when the weather changed, and the little beaches to the south sparkled in sunshine, we felt we'd had enough of sand in our shoes, sand trekked through the boat and drifted on the deck. And we stayed here, just one more day, all alone in this wonderful, inland world.

≈ 30 ≈
HARWOOD BAY

We were anchored in the back of Harwood Bay, loading the dinghy for a trip to shore, when we saw something crossing the harbour entrance.

"Killer whales," I said. But when I looked again, the shapes had turned into logs. They were long and black, silhouetted against the spindrift blowing down channel. And one of them moved, and something rose and fell.

"Kayakers," said Kristin, as they disappeared around the rocks in front of us.

We went berry picking in the woods and eventually came crashing out onto the beach one cove over from the boat. And in the hour we'd been gone, the kayakers had come ashore, had set up a tent and a camp, and had built a fire. They looked as though they'd been there forever.

Over the next day and a half, waiting for a break in the northwesterly winds, we got a glimpse into the life of the Little People. They took fresh-air baths in the shallow pool at the south end of the bay. They went trolling for dinner in Principe Channel. And when that didn't work, they invited us to a traditional kayakers' feast of home-jarred deer meat stew and giant biscuits stuffed with fruit and chocolate chips. We brought the coffee, and the four of us sat late into the evening, sprawled like lizards on the rocky beach.

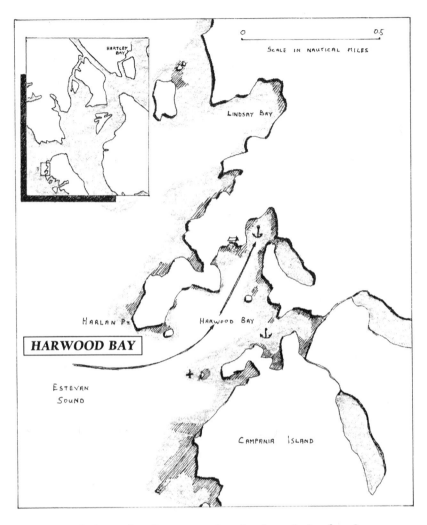

I envied them for the room they had, and the freedom to go anywhere at all. They'd camped a few days before at an ancient longhouse in a place so rocky and exposed that we've passed it five times now and not once been able to stop. And in the morning they put everything they had into the sleek boats designed and built by their own hands, and disappeared up the coast. They left nothing behind except for a few bits of charcoal and a circle of rocks, like the monument of a clan of tiny druids.

It was another two years before we were back in Harwood Bay. And somehow I expected to see them there again, as we came around the point and headed straight for the inner cove. But of course they weren't, and we dropped the anchor, put out a stern anchor, and loaded the dinghy for our trip to shore.

"You know," said Kristin. "I thought we'd see our friends in here again."

The *Sailing Directions* says: "Harwood Bay, 1.2 miles north of Anderson Passage, is open to the SW and too exposed for anchorage."

Though most of the bay is too deep for a pleasure boat to sit safely with its limited tackle, the little inner cove, reached through a narrow gap with reefs on the west side, shows depths of four to five fathoms. It is wonderfully sheltered from northwest winds, and we've sat here for days watching the swells heave in the channel. The salt lagoon to the east fills across a natural dam that floods only at the high tide.

We've also used Harwood Bay as a temporary shelter from southerly winds, tucking ourselves deep along the southern shore. There's a shallow place here at the mouths of three inner bays that fill on the rising tide. A stone wall runs across the westernmost of these inlets; from Harwood Bay it looks like a jumble of boulders until you notice the neatly made gap tunneled through the centre. The central bay leads inland to a saltwater lake and a small stream. The stream provides good drinking water, but it's a long hike from the bay and back.

Boats anchoring at this corner of Harwood Bay should watch for the rocks at the northern end of the shallows.

Despite its size, Harwood Bay can be hard to locate when approaching from the north. You have to get quite close to—or even beyond—Harlan Point before the entrance becomes apparent.

≈ 31 ≈
TROLLERS LAGOON

chart 3742

A very sheltered, very shallow bay on the north side of Otter Channel can be reached through a gap at its eastern end. I call this unnamed bay Trollers' Lagoon, for it is sometimes used by fishermen working the bottom end of Principe Channel. But a couple of creek watchers who often anchor here know the place as Bear Cove.

A white mooring float visible from Otter Channel first aroused our interest in the place. We tried twice, and gave up both times, before we pressed on through the narrow entrance and anchored off the north shore of the island that forms the bulk of the bay. We thought we might have been the first people to anchor here for years.

We walked along the island's shore, around a stony point and into a shallow cove. Our little black-and-white dog ran ahead, darting through long grass, snaking up and down the beach, and found a man salvaging wood from an old building site. I think he was more surprised than we were when he looked up and saw the animal racing across the shore. "I didn't know what the hell that was coming toward me," he said.

He had his boat grounded on a make-shift grid, power tools spread around him. He whistled as he worked, sang at night—as he rowed through the bay—a wonderful old shanty in a voice that rang like bells.

The inner cove of the island was once the site of a small settlement. Along the Pitt Island shore on the north side of the lagoon are

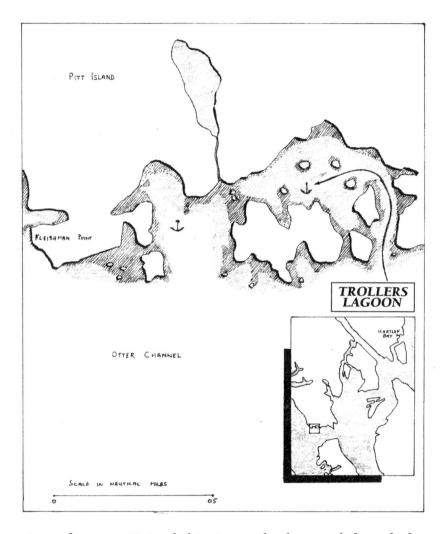

PITT ISLAND

FLEISHMAN POINT

TROLLERS
LAGOON

HARTLEY
BAY

OTTER CHANNEL

SCALE IN NAUTICAL MILES

0   0.5

signs of ancient Native habitation, and a bear trail through the woods. There is a small midden on the island's inner cove, and remnants of a more recent construction. According to the man doing salvage, there was once a European settlement there. But the creek watchers said it was a logging camp. At any rate, there's very little left.

The forest behind it is unusually open and pleasant for walking. We've seen no bears, but a deer so unused to people that it stood and watched us pass just sixty feet away, and then went back to its quiet browsing.

Trollers' Lagoon is entered through the easternmost gap in the group of islands. Pay close attention to chart 3742; there are several rocks and reefs off the entrance. Inside, the bay is freckled with rocky islets, and is quite shallow throughout. But the bottom varies from thick mud in places to shingled rock that doesn't take an anchor very well. Anchorage seems best in the broadest part of the bay; the area west of the small cove in the largest island is encumbered by rocks and reefs.

CURLEW BAY

chart 3742

I t's a forty-two-mile trip between Butedale and Lowe Inlet, a normal one-day passage for boats going north up the Inside Passage. For most, that's no more than a seven-hour day, often less. But for us, in a gaff-rigged sailboat with a small auxiliary, it's ten hours at best, closer to twelve on the average.

There aren't many places to stop between the two. We spent a night in the nook below Red Bluff Lake and rolled viciously in the wake of passing ships. We don't like Coghlan Anchorage; it's broad and windy. Access to attractive places in Union Passage—its northern end is a marine park—has to be timed with the tides. We've anchored along the shore of McKay Reach, in bays too small to be named, and almost lost the anchor when it jammed fiercely on a rocky bottom. It's no wonder that so many boats make the trip in one leap. And it's no wonder that we've fallen in love with Curlew Bay

Turning off at Wright Sound for the trip to Fin Island adds eight miles to the trip going in and another eight going out, but this sheltered bay known best by sports fishermen is more than worth the detour.

Our first time there, we took the standard advice and anchored deep in the bay between the shoulders of rock where the depth was less than five fathoms. As though to welcome us, a little bird perched on the boom, and rode in with us for the last half mile.

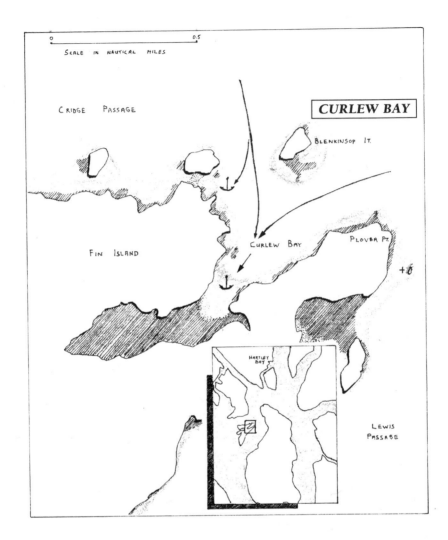

It was a pleasant spot. We had a salmon barbecue on the beach at the edge of the drying flats, walked the dog half a mile inland. But on our way out in the morning, a spit of shell and gravel at the entrance to Curlew Bay caught our attention, and the next year we didn't bother going any further than that.

The spit joins Fin Island to a small islet north of Curlew Bay. On normal tides, it doesn't quite disappear at high water. Though reefs extend northeast from Fin Island and southwest from the small islet, there's room to anchor between them, in about seven fathoms, without intruding on the entrance to the bay.

A log salvager sometimes uses Curlew Bay as a base, towing

in booms of logs in the evening and mooring them to the rocks further into the bay. But he's not there every night, nor every year, and we've never felt in anybody's way.

Occasionally, the beach is used by the Little People. The Fin Island end of the isthmus is higher and flatter, and a rough campsite is cleared among the trees there. It is, unfortunately, also used by some boaters as a garbage disposal site.

≈ 33 ≈
KOORYET BAY

chart 3741

Kooryet Bay, ten miles north from the bottom of Banks Island, is a convenient place for boats using Principe Channel. It's a bit exposed to northwest winds, and gusts can blow with surprising strength down through the hills to the west and southwest, but we've found Kooryet Bay more attractive than most of the neighbouring anchorages.

The *Sailing Directions* says: "Confined shelter for small craft can be found in its south end, clear of the shoal rocks. Local knowledge is required."

We tuck ourselves into the square cove right on the western shore. The stern anchor, set well off the beam, keeps us off the rocks to the south. Other boats anchor just about anywhere at the southern end of Kooryet Bay, but a large rock lies east of the narrowing bay leading south to vast tidal flats. The small curve of beach just west of the lagoon's outlet was cleared of rocks long ago for a canoe skidway.

We've tried anchoring at the northern end of the bay, off the wide stream that drains Kooryet Lake, but weren't happy with the results. The bottom rises steeply from more than thirteen fathoms to a shelf of drying rock, and a strong current flows through the gap between Banks Island and Kooryet Island.

But there are remains of a building on the point north of the stream mouth. And in late summer, when salmon swim up the

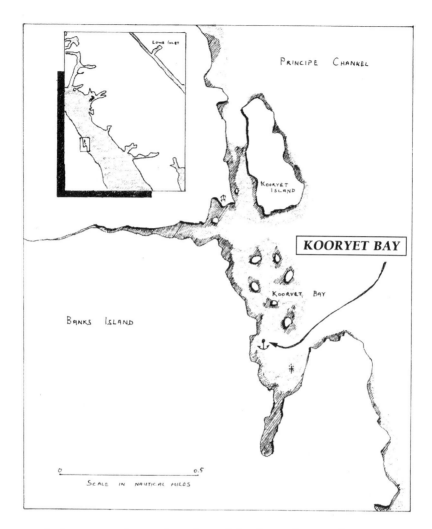

creek, large numbers of seals and birds gather at the entrance. We've rowed up the stream to the limit of the tide, and we've caught codfish from the dinghy at both ends of Kooryet Bay.

The shore of Banks Island tends to be rather featureless. When approaching this anchorage from the south, Joseph Hill serves as a convenient guide. Its conspicuous, domed peak is one mile west of the bay. From the north, the gap between Banks Island and Kooryet Island is obvious from a considerable distance.

≈ 34 ≈
BUCHAN INLET

We didn't have the close-up view of chart 3721 when we snuck into Buchan Inlet in search of a place where we'd be completely alone. The *Sailing Directions* didn't say much: "This inlet is only suitable for small craft." But from a look at chart 3741, we didn't think there would be many problems. "I bet nobody goes in there," I said. There was just one gap, so narrow that I couldn't touch a pencil point to the chart without covering both sides. "Probably not," said Kristin. "There's sure nobody out here."

We turned in past Tweedsmuir Point just minutes before high tide, cruised through the twisting passage to the tiny narrows. "It looks okay," said Kristin, on the bow. And the current caught us, and pulled us through.

Another boat, the first we'd seen in three days, sat at anchor in the very spot we'd picked out hours before.

It wasn't as beautiful as we'd hoped. But huge, orange jellyfish swam this way and that, and we poked among rocks covered with sealife. We might have stayed longer, if we weren't in a hurry to be home by September.

At low slack the next morning I hauled up the anchor, only to drop it again a moment later. My hands were covered with the long, red tendrils of poisonous jellyfish. They clung to the line in slimy clots, and they stang like nettles. I had to hurry

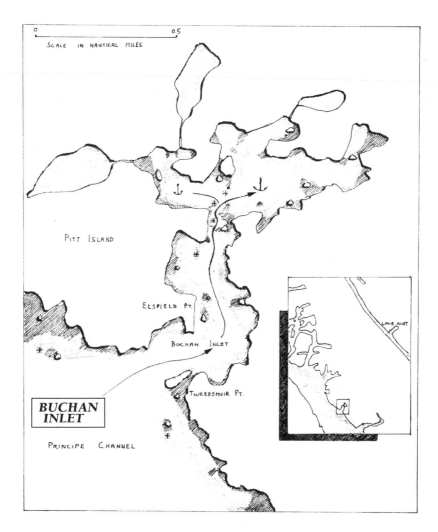

back to the cockpit, put on rubber gloves. Already the tide had turned against us.

Two men from the other boat scouted the narrow entrance in their dinghy. It looked okay, they said, except for one rock on the right side of the passage. But the current was building rapidly, rushing in swirls through the gap. I put the engine in gear, and headed out.

Kristin was on the bow. She saw the rock before I did, and shouted. It came gliding up the side, a big square thing as sharp edged as a steamer trunk. ("No, no," says Kristin now. "It was the size of a refrigerator. Maybe bigger.") And the current was pushing us straight toward it.

I couldn't see what was ahead. I jammed the throttle open,

heaved on the tiller. Kristin came down the deck a step at a time, then clutched the shrouds as she peered overboard. The rock disappeared under the curve of the bilge. And the bow came slowly round, water surging at the stem. I waited for the bang; it had to come. I imagined the propellor hitting rock, the sound that would make. It would be a horrible, expensive noise.

Then the current turned us the other way, tossed us sideways. I shoved the tiller over, and suddenly we were through the narrows.

It was the last time, we said, that we'd go through there without the detailed chart. But four years later we arrived at Buchan Inlet just before high tide. And, again, a boat was already in the place we wanted to be, snug against the shore in the cove west of the narrows.

"We'll go into the lagoon," I said. It was a completely different place at high tide. Our tortuous little channel had swelled into a broad passage dotted with small islets, but still we stopped the boat below the walls of cliff, and I rowed through in the dinghy.

I was back in a few minutes. I said, "It looks okay."

"Did you see the rock?" asked Kristin.

I shook my head. "It's under water."

"That huge thing?" she said, sounding doubtful. "Did you go all the way through?"

"Sure," I said, though I hadn't. The current had been so strong I was afraid I wouldn't get back out.

We rushed through the gap, faster and faster as the stream pulled us along. There was kelp on one side, rocks on the other, and just when we thought we were through, another rock loomed up on the bow.

It was just a guess which way to go. But I turned the boat to the east, and we came gliding into the main lagoon. It was sheltered in there; though the wind blew quite hard on the outside, it passed over the trees with a low, moaning hum. There were otters playing on the island off the stern, gulls squawking in huge circles above us. And I wrote in the log:

"We've been into the lagoon twice now, and Kristin says there won't be a third time until we get the detailed chart."

If entering Buchan Inlet:

~ Wait for high slack before going through the narrows.

~ Watch for the large, ugly rock that lies on the west side of the gap, and the others inside, on each side of the channel.

~ Bring a pair of rubber gloves. And don't forget the chart.

≈ 35 ≈
PATTERSON INLET

chart 3741/3721

We seem to be always going off on some wild goose chase or another. One year we hunted for an abandoned airstrip that we'd been told lay decomposing in the bush—machinery and equipment intact after almost fifty years. The next we were hiking through high hills for a forgotten town that we never found. And then we sailed up Patterson Inlet, looking for an ancient Native village that supposedly stood at its head.

And all we found was a logging operation that we'd never heard of before.

Patterson is typical of the coastal inlets: long and narrow, steep right to the head. It's a bit unusual in that it's a two-headed inlet, neatly divided by a long, thick spit. The logging operation had set up in the south arm; a road climbed up into the hills beyond the inlet. We anchored in the north arm, reached through a clear but narrow passage, in a round bay with a good, muddy bottom.

Moolock Cove, part of Mink Trap Bay, nearly pushes through the northern wall of Patterson Inlet. It's attractive there, with the thinnest spit dividing the two anchorages, but the bottom drops off very quickly, reaching nearly 360 feet two cables from the shore.

If there ever was a village in Patterson Inlet, we could see no signs of it.

Entrance is simple to Patterson Inlet, the current not substantially strong. Crab traps are sometimes set in the channel.

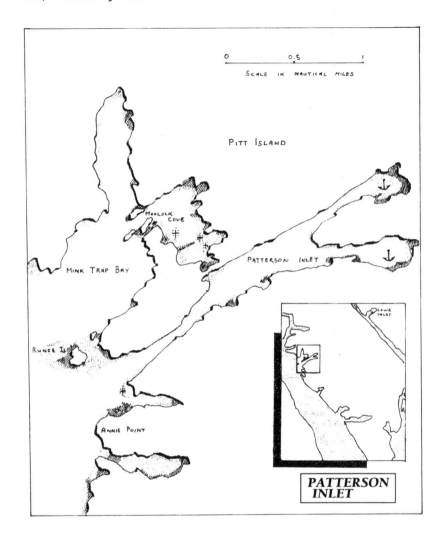

PATTERSON INLET

Anchorage is also possible in the narrow cove between Patterson Inlet and Annie Point. It's a gloomy, steep-sided gap in the rocks, filled with bugs. Too exposed for any night with a westerly or northwesterly wind, it does have a good creek at its head.

I walked the dog over the little beach at the back, only to hurry back to the boat when something growled at us from the trees. As we headed out, I saw the animal swimming across the entrance, from one point to another. "Look," I said to Kristin. "A pig. A swimming pig."

It must have been the way its hair spread on the water that made me see that. We watched it clamber out onto the rocks, and shake itself: a big, sleek coyote.

≈ 36 ≈
LOWE INLET

chart 3772

Lowe Inlet is fourteen miles north of the bottom of Grenville Channel, a bit more than forty miles from Butedale. It's one of the regular stops on the Inside Passage, and though sometimes quite crowded with cruising boats, it's also one of the most attractive.

At its head the Kumowdah River tumbles over a rocky ledge and swirls through a lower pool that shrinks and grows with the tide. Late in the summer spawning salmon gather in the pool, struggling up Verney Falls on their way to their spawning beds. There can be hundreds of them in there at a time, some waiting for the spring tides to lessen the jump, others just leaping blindly into the roaring falls and tumbling back again. It's a useless gesture, but I don't think it's due to stupidity; hordes of seals come to feast in that surging pool.

Late one August I saw a black bear fishing from the rocks beside the falls, snatching clumsily at the flying salmon. But according to creek watchers, it's a rare sight.

The pool is closed to sports fishing. But cruisers bring their skiffs and dinghies right inside, watching as fish bubble up from the base of the falls and fling themselves into the water, onto the rocks, just about everywhere. I've spent an hour there and not seen one make it over the top. But every year, salmon by the thousands top Verney Falls only to find, beyond the string of lakes behind Lowe Inlet, another waterfall nearly ten times as high.

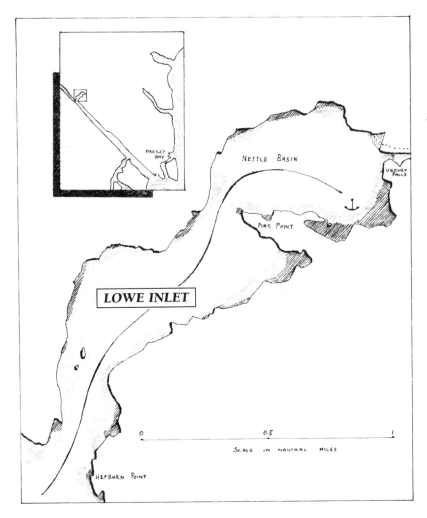

Carved into the north shore of Nettle Basin, Verney Falls is the most appealing feature of Lowe Inlet, and most boats head straight for it. They usually fan themselves out along the shore in both directions, anchoring in a curved line a comfortable distance from the drying flats. But at least one cruising guide encourages boats to anchor right in the river current, as close to the falls as they can get. I'm sure that puts them in the most scenic spot, but it always strikes me as unfair to others; it's rather like going to a drive-in movie and having a great ugly bread truck park in front of you.

Hating crowds, and the leap-frog game that always goes on in places like this, we anchor on the opposite shore, below the peninsula that forms Nettle Basin. There's a house in the woods there, a little

A black bear fishes at Verney Falls in Lowe Inlet.

cove in the basin's southwest corner that fills with the tide and runs inland to old pilings. And there's better shelter. When it's blowing in Grenville Channel, Lowe Inlet can generate its own special winds, with strong gusts that swirl down from the mountains and in through the gap above Pike Point. It can whip small whitecaps in the inner harbour, blow straight up the mouth of Kumowdah River. We've sat happily off the little islet southeast of the peninsula and watched half the cruising fleet re-set their anchors one after another.

But Lowe Inlet is a good, safe harbour. The entrance is clear, though caution is needed when entering from the north. A rocky reef juts into Grenville Channel, and the tide can do funny things at the mouth of the inlet, particularly on the ebb.

Inside Hepburn Point, the fairway narrows in two places to a cable's length or less. Watch for reefs extending south toward Don Point, and for shallow ledges on both sides of the entrance to Nettle Basin.

There are ruins of a cannery on the north side of the basin, recent logging behind them. And on the eastern shore, just north of the river mouth, are the remains of ancient fish traps.

A trail leads up from there, on the north bank of Kumowdah River, to a series of lakes and sandy beaches. The water is warm enough for a chilly swim, the scenery magnificent. No matter how many boats are anchored in the inlet, it's not likely to be crowded at the lakes; a lot of people don't go to shore at all.

Keep clear of the drying flats filling the southern bays of Nettle Basin. And watch for bears; grizzlies have been seen at this mainland inlet.

This popular anchorage and surrounding shore is now preserved as Lowe Inlet Marine Park. It encompasses an area of 767 hectares, but the land on both sides of the Kumowdah River is an Native Reserve. The logged-off section of shore is not part of the park.

≈ 37 ≈

KLEWNUGGIT INLET

chart 3772

Halfway through Grenville Channel, Klewnuggit Inlet pokes long fingers into the steep hills of the mainland coast. It's a beautiful place, though somehow far less popular than Lowe Inlet nine miles to the south.

Tides enter Grenville Channel from each end and meet near Klewnuggit. The *Sailing Directions* says the flood tides join at Evening Point while the ebbs meet a mile to the north, though both can vary according to wind conditions. When approaching from the south, give a wide berth to Morning Reef and pass Rogers Point before turning in to Klewnuggit.

The closest anchorage is in the first finger: called Ship Anchorage on the chart. The inlet is fairly deep, so we anchor off the tiny cove east of Harriot Island. Submerged and drying rocks lie close to the southeast, but there's lots of room behind them. At high tide we've passed through the passage north of Harriot Island, but the route is not recommended by the *Sailing Directions*, which says shoal rocks lie within it. Sometimes, it can be thick with kelp.

East Inlet, with small-craft anchorages at each of its double heads, is often recommended as the best and most scenic spot in Klewnuggit. But it's an extra three miles in—and another three miles out—right to the top of East Inlet.

Ironically, everything *except* Ship Anchorage—and Exposed Inlet—is included in the borders of Klewnuggit Inlet Marine

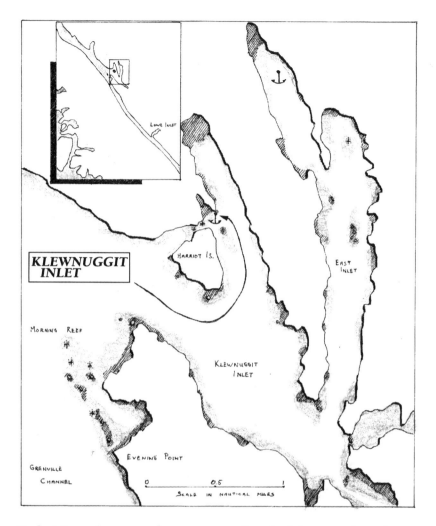

KLEWNUGGIT INLET

Park. Measuring more than seventeen hundred hectares, it embraces all of Freda Lake. It's western boundary runs down the middle of the peninsula separating East Inlet from Ship Anchorage.

Freda Lake, draining through a lower pool down a series of waterfalls, is noted for spectacular hiking.

GIBSON ISLAND

chart 3773

I was working on the boat, replacing porthole gaskets, when a trimaran came sailing into the bay. It ghosted along, crossed the open circle in the cabin side, moved with no wind at all like a small, yachty Flying Dutchman. And it anchored off the end of the dock, floated there with the sun sparkling on acres of deck.

There were two wonderful people on board, and a small dog, and they reminded me a lot of friends we'd had when we first started sailing. I lent them a packet of charts, aimed them toward a few interesting places. And when they came back two weeks later, there was a new spot marked for me at the top of Grenville Channel.

It was a place I'd passed at least a dozen times; there was even an anchor printed on the chart. But I'd never noticed it at all, this bay at the south side of Gibson Island, this place called Gunboat Harbour.

The *Sailing Directions* gives it a short paragraph: "Gunboat Harbour lies between the SE side of Gibson Island and Bloxam Island. It affords temporary anchorage to small vessels in about 3 fathoms (5.5 metres) off the drying flat near its head."

Gibson Island lies in the mouth of the Skeena River, right at the top of Grenville Channel. The harbour was empty when I stopped there late in August, on my way home up the Inside Passage. All along its edge, like a dotted line drawn on the water,

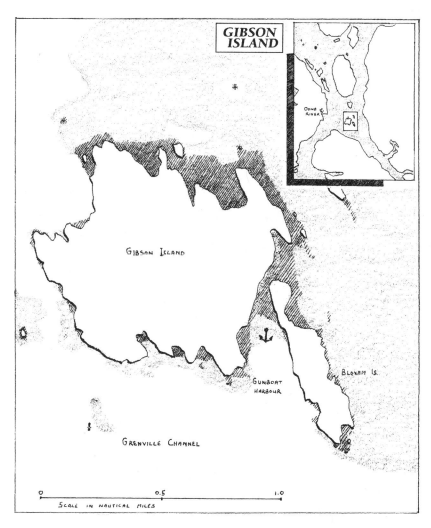

GIBSON ISLAND

GIBSON ISLAND

OONA RIVER

GIBSON ISLAND

GUNBOAT HARBOUR

BLOXAM IS.

GRENVILLE CHANNEL

0   0.5   1.0

SCALE IN NAUTICAL MILES

strands of bull kelp neatly defined the anchorage.

There was a nice beach along the shore of Gibson Island, a low-lying forest behind it where old, shingled trees grew from swampy ground. They were short and well spaced, with their branches bunched near the top like a garden of enormous flowers. They swayed in the northwest wind with an eerie, creaking groan.

At low tide I crossed the gap north of Bloxam Island and followed the shore north up Gibson Island. It's a place well suited for the Little People, something different from most of our anchorages. Instead of the usual piles of driftwood, the beaches collect whole trees washed down from the river. Some have been stranded here so long that saplings have taken root on stumps and rotting trunks.

Stranded logs sprout new growth on the beaches of Gunboat Harbour.

The river flows by, silty and green. For more than a mile to the east, the water is less than three fathoms deep, the start of a series of sand-and-gravel bars that stretch up the Skeena. And on summer mornings the river brings fog to Gibson Island.

I woke to it: a fog so thick I couldn't see a thing beyond the edge of the deck. I could hear the bell buoy on the shallow spot to the southeast, the hoot of passing boats and the rumble of engines. It cleared late in the morning, only to come rushing back down the river a few hours later. But by then I was already north at the entrance to Kelp Passage, chased out by a forecast for southeast gales.

It was tempting to stay. But Gunboat Harbour is open to the south, to the winds funnelling up the forty-mile length of Grenville Channel. And when I switched on the radio in the morning, I was glad I'd left. The bell buoy had been swept off the shallows and had vanished somewhere at the river mouth.

≈ 39 ≈

NEWCOMBE HARBOUR

chart 3746/3753

Petrel Channel provides a convenient shortcut between Principe and Ogden channels. It offers boats an alternative to the open-water route outside McCauley Island and through the overfalls at the end of Browning Entrance. Shorter by five miles than the outside route, Petrel Channel can save considerable travelling time when a boat gets the three-knot tide behind it.

Winds can whip through the valleys of McCauley Island, churning whitecaps on the east-west portion of Petrel Channel, but the passage is infinitely more sheltered than the outer route.

Newcombe Harbour is about seven miles up from the channel's south end. It's a good place to wait out a change in the tides, or to stop after a late, southbound trip through the narrowest parts of the channel.

Watch for the entrance if the tide is running; you have to be quite close before the channel is apparent. The entrance is partially blocked by a shoal extending from McCutcheon Point, so keep toward the south shore.

The *Sailing Directions* advises boats to anchor a mile from the entrance, in the basin south of a prominent point and a small islet.

A better spot is in the small cove on the south shore half a mile into the harbour. A heavy cable may still be attached to the rocks off the little islet in the bay, a convenient place to tie a shore line.

There is a pleasant beach of grass and rock here, a nice stream trickling down from the forest.

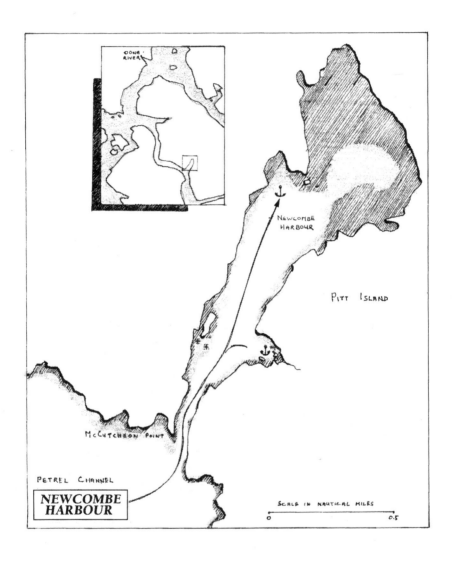

OONA RIVER

NEWCOMBE
HARBOUR

PITT ISLAND

McCUTCHEON POINT

PETREL CHANNEL

**NEWCOMBE
HARBOUR**

SCALE IN NAUTICAL MILES

0   0.5

≈ 40 ≈
CAPTAIN COVE

chart 3746/3753

We've stopped many times at Captain Cove. We've felt our way in through the fog, sailed in on lovely westerlies. Once we flew in with the motor screaming, the whole boat stinking of sulphur, anxious to get the anchor down and the dinghy launched before the overcharged batteries exploded beneath our feet.

Whether staying for the night or just waiting for a tide change in Petrel Channel, we can hope to see deer and bears at Captain Cove, and there's always a flock of seabirds perched like eagles in a prominent tree. A good, safe anchorage, it's one we return to again and again.

There's a detailed view of Captain Cove on chart 3753, but you don't really need it. The entrance is apparent from a long way off and the harbour, for the most part, is free of dangers. It can be windy at times, but anchorage is good in any of its three shallow bays. We prefer the little cove formed by a chain of islets, but so do most other boats. There's not room for more than two or three in there, but it's a big harbour.

Other preferred anchorages are just south of the last islet in the chain, up against the pair of islets deep on the south shore, and along the fringe of the drying flats above and below the logging road pushed through the eastern shore. There are often crab traps all through the bay, and boaters should watch for

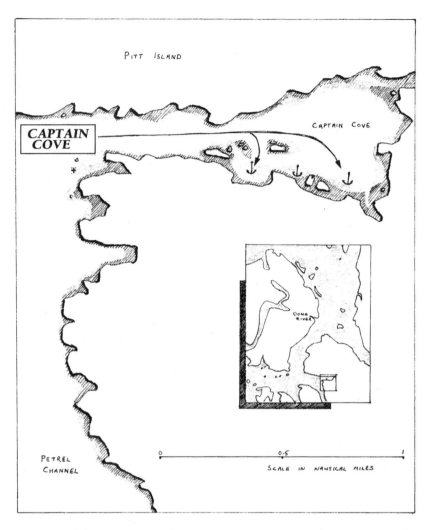

make-shift floats; some of them can easily be confused with ordinary flotsam.

Broad valleys lead inland up both coves at the head of the harbour. Look for huge moonsnails on the mudflats, and culturally modified trees at the forest edge; one or two have been hollowed and burned in the manner of ancient logging. There are also some interesting ruins among the trees behind the two linked islets close to shore. Unfortunately the woods here are sometimes used as a garbage dump by some unscrupulous boaters.

We chose Captain Cove to sit out a rare summer gale one year, coming almost ten miles to anchor in the five-fathom spot on the south shore. It was a southeaster, just building as we slipped in between the islets. Gusts came from every direction and we circled round and round, put down the anchor and picked it up again, circled back the other way.

"Just anchor," said Kristin, laughing. "You look like an old dog arranging his little bed."

So we anchored with our stern to the west, fifty feet of chain and one hundred and twenty feet of rope streamed out over the shallow bottom. And when the wind came moaning down through the mountain valley, swirling east to west through the harbour, we hung forty pounds of lead on the rode, and settled in for the night.

The gale arrived before midnight; winds of forty knots measured at Bonilla Island. But the gusts were far more than that as they blasted through the mountains and came roaring through the trees. They sent us hurling back on the anchor line, stretching taut all that lead and chain, heeling so far that pencils and books tumbled from the counter tops.

Then the gust would ease and we'd spring forward on the lead and chain, hear the wind rise again and rush toward us. And back we'd go with the shoreline spinning past. I stood looking out a porthole as the boat yawed and tipped; and I saw nothing but black water just inches away.

But we'd picked a good spot at Captain Cove. The anchor burrowed into the mud like a big steel clam. And we didn't move an inch.

≈ 41 ≈
LAWSON HARBOUR

chart 3927/3956

The site of a once-thriving community, Lawson Harbour lies in the middle of Arthur Passage, just twenty miles from Prince Rupert. Though it offers good shelter from southeast winds, reefs lie on both sides of the entrance, and chart 3927 does not display the harbour in great detail.

Boats must go well into Bloxam Pass before turning south into the harbour; a submerged rock sits northwest of Break Island. The limits of the harbour are best defined at low tide. A large reef juts out from the western shore, extending northeast from the little islet where a curious rock formation stands like a child's fort.

When the winds are strong from the south, we nestle up toward the shelving beach, off the pilings from a ruined boat shed. The *Sailing Directions* says anchorage is best further out, just 0.1 miles south of the entrance.

There are remains of several buildings in the trees behind the curve of beach. The village at one time even had its own school. We've found a few old bottles in the mud, a brass razor among the stones.

In Chalmers Anchorage, just to the north, an excellent beach forms the western edge of a fair-weather alternative to Lawson Harbour. In its thick sand we've often seen the footprints of wolves and deer: only rarely those of people.

Chalmers Anchorage is an exposed, deep-water harbour just

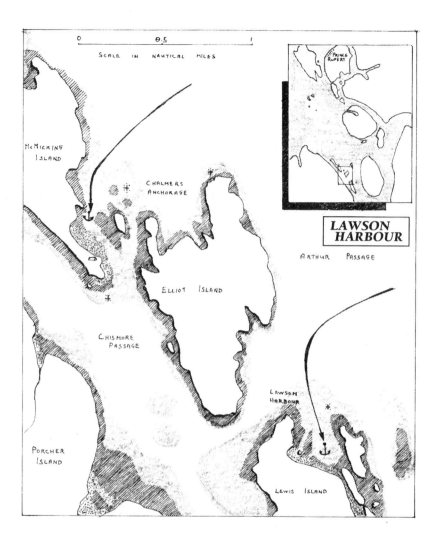

west of Francis Point. With a range of depth from eleven to twenty-four fathoms, it's not a desirable place for most cruisers. But small boats can anchor behind the reefs and islets between McMicking and Elliott islands, in a sandy channel that gives little room for error.

The tide is strong through here—ebbing north and flooding south—and the reefs extend far from the little islets in all directions. In addition, northwest winds bend around the shore of McMicking Island and blow right through the harbour. And the wakes of passing cruise ships set a boat on its beam ends.

But this spot has become a favourite for us on the last night of our journeys. One of the finest beaches on the north coast, it's close enough to home that we can see the lights of the Ridley

At low tide, the beach is immense in Chalmers Anchorage. The high tide will come nearly to the stumps in the foreground.

Island superport; far enough out that we've still got a half day's travel ahead of us. And the broad stretch of sand is a great place for our last salmon dinner of the summer.

We met one of the Little People on this beach, huddled below the limbs of a furry tree. He waded out on the morning tide and caught crabs with his bare hands among the eel grass. In the centre of the beach were signs that others had been here too—a tent clearing on a mossy glade; an arrangement of logs and boards in the curious manner of the Little People.

In the summer of '94, strips of red survey tape appeared suddenly along the sand. They fluttered from tree branches, from bushes and stumps, marked in felt pen with numbers and codes. And up in the woods, trees had been marked with blotches of orange spray paint, like targets, for future cutting. Though the island was selectively logged years ago, it seems it may not be quite so entrancing in another year or two.

At high tide the anchorage can be approached from either direction. The easiest route is from the north, staying close to the McMicking shore. Anchoring at a comfortable distance south of the prominent point on McMicking Island keeps you at a safe distance from the reefs. The sounder should show about forty feet; remember that chart 3956 is METRIC. We always put down two anchors in this limited spot.

≈ 42 ≈
LARSEN HARBOUR

chart 3747

There are few places more inhospitable than the northwest tip of Banks Island. The water is shallow far from shore, the coast strewn with rocks and wicked reefs, with big patches of kelp that don't always stay anchored where they should. It's where you'll find Deadman Inlet and Deadman Islet. A cheery little place that. Larsen Harbour is right on the tip, actually on an island separated from Banks by a twisting gap that floods at high tide. It's protected to the northwest by a chain of islands and reefs, to the west and south by the bulk of Larsen Island. There are six mooring buoys in the harbour, little room for anything else.

It was an eight-mile crossing from the bottom of Dolphin Island, a wild sail in a northwesterly blowing at twenty-four knots. We plunged and tossed through the swells, flinging up clouds of spray and digging the bowsprit in the waves.

Half a mile off Larsen Harbour the bottom shallowed to four fathoms. Surf crashed on the offshore islands. A moderate swell washed up on the rocks at the harbour entrance, and bounced back to form high crests and deep holes across the channel. We took down the sails and motored in, puttering past reefs that appeared and disappeared in the swell. We could smell the surf roaring on every side. And we picked up the third mooring buoy, two hours after leaving Dolphin Island.

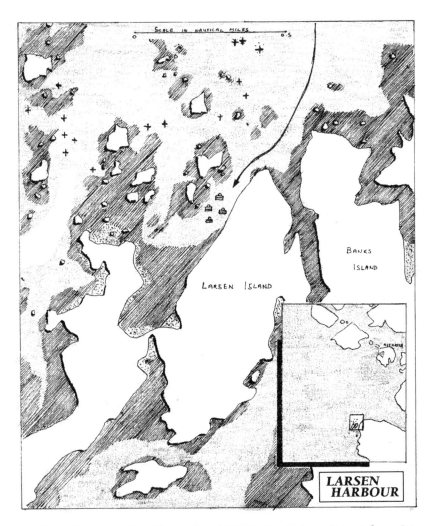

"I might as well tell you," said Kristin. "I hated it. I found it frightening, uncomfortable, dangerous and inconvenient."

"What?" I said. "Inconvenient?"

Today, I'm not sure why we were there. We had a vague idea of going south down Hecate Strait, standing offshore all the way to Port Hardy. But in the morning we cast off from the mooring buoy and scooted round the north shore of Banks, right past Deadman Islet to the sheltered waters of Principe Channel.

"Larsen Harbour," says the *Sailing Directions*, "is between the north side of Larsen Island and the islands and drying reefs to the NW. It is only suitable for small craft and local knowledge is advised."

It also gives precise directions for entering the harbour: "The approach is between Larsen Harbour light and the drying reefs 0.1 mile west. Heavy kelp grows on the 4 fathom (7.3 metres) bank in the approach to the harbour."

Under no condition should the harbour be even approached without proper charts. The entrance can be dangerous in even moderate winds. A note on the chart in the general area says, "Tides very variable about here."

Two days after we anchored in Larsen Harbour, our little diesel gave up the ghost. Had it happened as we sat rocking in the waves and swells among those reefs . . .

"Have you thought of that?" said Kristin. "Hmmm? Have you thought of that?"

≈ 43 ≈
BILLY BAY

chart 3761

Billy Bay is a sad place. The remains of dreams lie scattered through the trees like the party hats and whistles of an abandoned New Year's dance. So many people have tried here—and all have lost—that the land almost smells of gloom. Billy Bay, at the bottom of Porcher Island, is named for a man who homesteaded in the river valley above the bay. You can still see his fields, his vast dike and the remains of a wooden watercourse that drained the land and held back the river. You can see his cabin, or the last few logs of it, hidden in the trees. You can see the years of work that went into it, back-breaking and endless.

Billy was Japanese. In 1942, he was rounded up as an enemy to the country and shipped off to an inland camp.

There were people here long before Billy. The bay and its off-lying islets carry signs of habitation that pre-date the Pyramids. And there were people here after Billy; their collapsing sheds and burned-out homes stand along both sides of the river. But Billy may always be here. They say you can see his ghost some mornings, like a wisp of dew, walking atop his crumbling dike.

Several hidden rocks guard the entrance to Billy Bay. The best approach is on a route heading straight for the entrance of the next bay to the east. Keep going until you are past the rocks lying off to port, then follow the shore into Billy Bay. Watch for crab-trap floats.

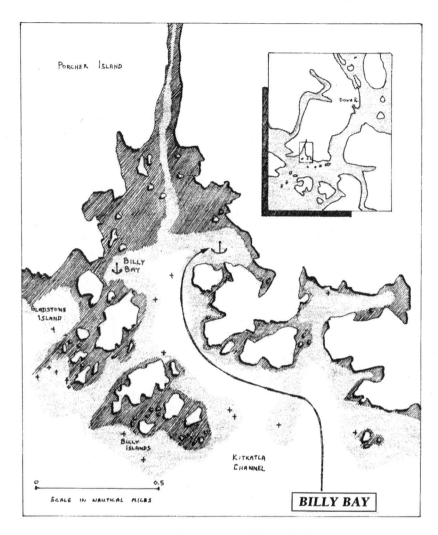

BILLY BAY

The bay dries out within two cables of the entrance. But a small cove in the eastern portion has good anchorage in two to four fathoms, mud bottom. With a good creek just to the north, it's the best spot in the bay, particularly during southerly winds. But the southwest corner of Billy Bay offers a more scenic anchorage off a nice little beach. The basin below it—shown as one fathom on the chart—is confined by reefs on the south shore.

A walk up the Billy River is like discovering an ancient civilisation. You see the first relics where the bay narrows to a river mouth, barnacle-covered on the stream bed—a battery and swim goggles wrapped in codline—then motor parts and scraps of metal, more and more the further you go—an electrical box,

The old sawmill at Billy Bay is slowly falling from its pilings.

bits of cable and hose. You come to the first building—a sawmill collapsing on its stilt legs—stumble on an overturned tractor, scattered saw blades and machine belts. Everywhere there are coils and tangles of rope, as though these forgotten people had everything lashed in place.

And at each little homesite, each burned-down foundation, there's something left behind. Something very sad.

A carpet sweeper pokes a bright blue handle from charred rubble; flower baskets sprout masses of weeds; elaborate crib-work pokes from a crumbling dike, like dinosaur bones. And in a garden below a boardwalk, forgotten in a grove of trees, a child's red-painted swing dangles from a branch, and rocks only in a breeze.

≈ 44 ≈
KITKATLA INLET – CESSFORD ISLANDS

chart 3927/3761

Anchored off the old dolphins at a gravel quarry in the corner of the inlet," I wrote in our log. "The moon, still four nights from full, has risen over the trees behind us and a line of clouds, grey and purple and silvered at the edge, is slowly washing over it. Across the northern horizon the sky is flickering with northern lights, pale green bands and vertical rods. All around the boat things are splashing and rippling at the water; further off, a seal is huffing on the surface. Far away, a wolf is howling."

It was our first night in Kitkatla Inlet. We'd gone straight to the southwest corner, where Porcher Island narrows to less than half a mile. On the other side of the isthmus was a long sweep of stony beach, right on the edge of Hecate Strait. But the bush was too thick for walking. If we wanted to visit the outside beaches, we'd have to travel east first, and then north and west again, in a loop of nearly fifty miles to Welcome Harbour, just seven miles from where we'd started.

We moved back toward the entrance of the inlet and anchored in a bay among the sand-speckled Cessford Islands. It's possible to slip in from the east, just north of the chunk of rock off the largest island, but the dangers are usually hidden, and the current is strong in the narrows between Kitkatla Channel and Kitkatla Inlet. It's better to approach the area from the northwest.

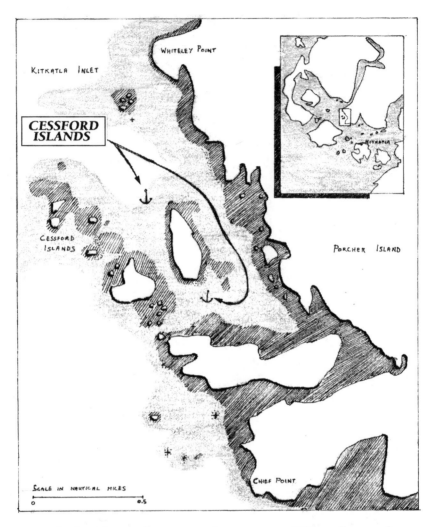

At high tide our bay seemed enormous. When the southeast winds picked up, it seemed a terrible place.

Kitkatla Inlet lies on a slant from southeast to northwest. Southeasters, usually the strongest of northcoast winds, blow right up its length. Even in the summer they can sometimes reach full gale force, and steep waves roll up the length of the shallow inlet.

Soon we had whitecaps in our anchorage; the low land ahead offered little shelter. The boat heeled in the gusts, then snubbed up on the two anchors with a creak of rope. We rode it out, all twenty hours of it, but the next southeaster found us one island back, in a calm spot with the wind whistling on each side, and

Kristin stands on the bow, watching for rocks as we enter a northcoast inlet.

we sat there like a bit of wood resting in the eddies behind a river rock.

When the weather calmed, we went exploring. The entire inlet is rich with archaeological sites; Kitkatla Village on nearby Dolphin Island is the oldest inhabited site on the coast. We found thick shell middens, a house depression overgrown with devil's club, trees scarred by axes and fire.

We collected water from a muskeg stream, and startled a flock of swans at its head. And then the summer winds came up, the northwesterlies, and we moved back inside the bay as the process began all over again.

≈ 45 ≈
KITKATLA INLET – PHOENIX ISLANDS

chart 3927/3761

At the eastern end of Kitkatla Inlet, a long arm reaches right into the centre of Porcher Island. The channel is narrow and curved, and the tide stream reaches seven knots on the springs.

Near the mouth of the channel, on its north side, a pair of islands forms a sheltered anchorage in depths of two to four fathoms.

Though a twisting passage leads through the reefs at the east end of the anchorage, it is far too intricate for safe navigation. The entrance lies at the other end, either north of the Snass Islands or between them and the Phoenix Islands. There are a few rocks and reefs in the approach to the area, but they are all marked clearly on the charts. A tidal stream flows through the anchorage.

There is a wonderful stone fishtrap on the north side of the anchorage. The stone walls are almost buried by silt, and thousands of shore crabs prowl among them when the tide is out.

Phoenix Creek is a salmon stream. We sat on the rocks at its mouth, watching the fish pooling there as the tide came in. They settled lazily among the rocks, and I said how easy it would be to pick one up in the landing net. I even had it with me, lying in the bottom of the dinghy.

"No," said Kristin. "It wouldn't be fair."

Their journey was almost over. There are no bears on Porcher Island; we saw no signs of wolves. In one more tide, they'd be home.

"Just leave them," she said. "They've come a long way."

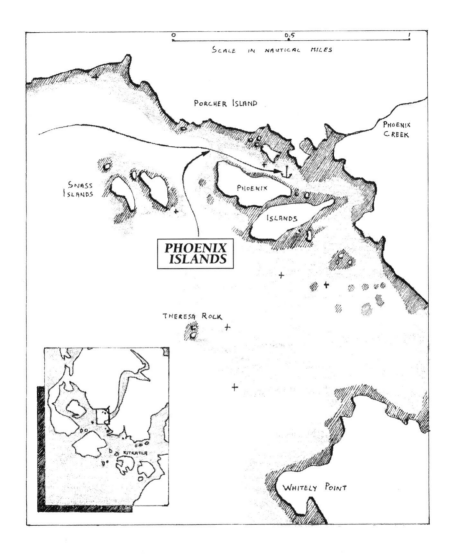

≈ 46 ≈
WELCOME HARBOUR

chart 3956/3909

A bout twenty miles from Prince Rupert, on the edge of Hecate Strait, is Welcome Harbour. It's a popular destination for boaters from the north coast city, a sort of gathering place on summer weekends. For sportsfishermen, it's a convenient anchorage after a day's trolling in nearby waters. Edye Passage, right at the harbour's entrance, is one of the best fishing spots in Chatham Sound.

The *Sailing Directions* is unusually eloquent: "This harbour does not offer a welcome to the stranger, being obstructed by numerous drying reefs and below-water rocks."

The large-scale, close-up view of chart 3909 (or older chart 3980) is the best guide available. Summer kelp blooming from rocks and reefs helps define the passage down past Dancey Island, but it's not an infallible guide. Every summer, it seems, at least one boat ends up on the rocks somewhere in Welcome Harbour. South and west of Dancey Island, a chain of rocky islets effectively divides the harbour into two separate areas. Boats can negotiate either of two intricate passages through the maze, but most don't bother going that far into Welcome Harbour. They head straight for the beach opposite Secret Cove, where a beautiful camping and picnic spot has been developed by the B.C. Forest Service and the Prince Rupert Sailing Association.

There's a good firepit, a pair of picnic tables, and an out-

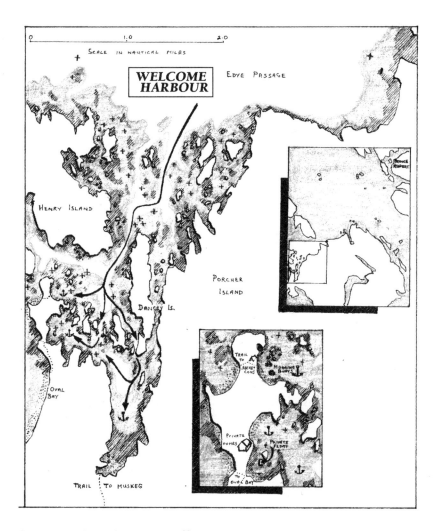

house tucked demurely off to one side. A guest book on a covered shelf invites visitors' comments, though it goes largely unfilled. Some people stay a week or more, pitching tents in moss-covered clearings, but drinking water is not supplied, and very hard to find.

A trail crosses from the campsite to Secret Cove, emerging at a steep bluff of loose gravel. A rope has been put in place for a handhold, and the cliff is not much of an obstacle to anyone in average condition.

From Secret Cove it's possible to follow the beaches south into Oval Bay. Short trails by-pass Welcome Point and other headlands, and the beach changes gradually from stones to

The schooner Rupert Pelican *lies at a mooring buoy off the Forest Service campground in Welcome Harbour.*

gravel to sand as it progresses to the south, so the walking gets easier, but can still be tiring.

Oval Bay is open to the west, pounded by the surf of prevailing summer winds. Wonderful things can appear here, from glass balls to stalks of bamboo, from Nike shoes to little black camera bags. (I still use mine, though I had to cut through the lining to shake out all the grains of sand.) It's a huge beach, stretching in an arc four miles from Welcome Point to Oval Point, and continuing south from there right to the bottom of Porcher Island.

At the campsite two orange mooring buoys are available for anyone's use. Other boats frequently anchor right among them and off slightly to the east. But mariners should note that a passage leading through from Secret Cove—a narrow, winding channel—brings fishboats almost into the mooring cove on their way through Welcome Harbour.

These boats coming in from Oval Bay often continue south through the maze of islets to the southern portion of Welcome Harbour. A Prince Rupert fishing family owns private property there on the bay that carves a narrow isthmus into Porcher Island. Though he has experienced some vandalism and disregard in the past, Harold Campbell still offers boaters access to his bay and use of the trails that cross his property to Oval Beach. The trails begin south of the buildings, in the corner of the Campbell's inner bay, at a spot marked with a couple of net floats. On summery weekends this part of Welcome Harbour can be very crowded.

"We had thirty-nine boats in here one Easter," says Campbell. "You could just about walk to the beach across their decks."

But there is a place much less visited in the large bay at the very southern end of the harbour. An old road begins at the south-west tip of the drying flats and climbs gently into the muskeg of Porcher Island. Some people bring their dinghies on the rising tide right to the little islets just north of the crumbling embankment that marks the beginning of the road. The shore here has been transformed into a series of pools, arranged in steps and shaped by stone walls, like a huge and elaborate rock garden.

Southeast winds howl down through the low hills above this bay, so this southern portion of Welcome Harbour should not be used in adverse weather.

≈ 47 ≈
KINAHAN ISLANDS

chart 3957/3958/3701

Fishermen sometimes use the Kinahan Islands as an anchorage, but never in southeast winds. The two main islands, imaginatively named East Kinahan Island and West Kinahan Island, form a wide-mouthed bay open to the south. They give good shelter to summer northwesterlies, though, and the mud-bottomed harbour is shallow enough to anchor just about anywhere north of the reefs off South Kinahan Island.

During spring tides the north-going ebb flows between the islands and over the ledge between them, as though through a funnel. Huge amounts of driftwood collect on the beaches, choking them from the tide line right to the trees.

West Kinahan Island is the site of a Second World War observation post. In the drying bay at its south end, enclosed by Little Kinahan Island, are elaborate earthworks and a grove of apple trees bearing small but sweet fruit in late summer. In the woods around them are rotting animal pens. We've been told it once was a fox farm, but some people say there was a mink farm there. Maybe both stories are right, and one stock somehow got loose among the other. But at any rate all the animals are gone. And now a heavy deer population roams through the islands.

Beaches on the two main islands are not too hospitable for kayakers, though fields around the old orchard are attractive and broad and padded with grass. The Little People may find an alternative

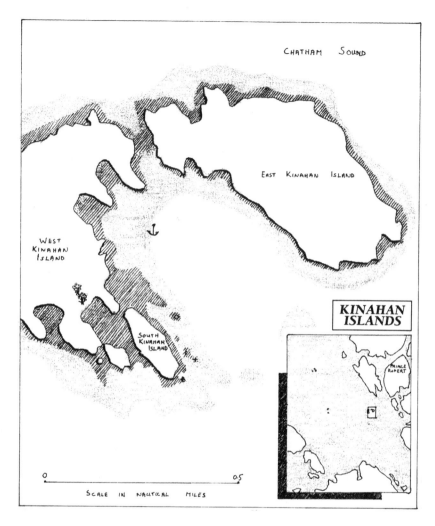

site at Kitson Island Marine Park, south of the Kinahans at the mouth of the Skeena. Kitson Island, with little Kitson Islet to the northeast, lies more than a mile from the nearest land. But it sits at the bottom of Flora Bank, a vast expanse of sand and gravel that dries, on tides nearing zero, all the way to the mouth of Porpoise Harbour. In the summer, we've seen seals gathering here for the Skeena salmon runs, hauled out on the low-tide sand like fishboats waiting for an opening.

48

LUCY ISLANDS

chart 3957/3985

The Lucy Islands group, off the northern entrance to Prince Rupert Harbour, is the one spot we always recommend to boaters going north, and especially to the Little People. There's a quiet lagoon enclosed by sandy beaches, a fascinating world of reefs and wooded islands. It's a place we always compared to a Caribbean atoll—until we took my sister and her husband out there.

They'd been to the Bahamas just the year before.

I looked along the beach as though I owned it. I held out my arms. "It looks like a Caribbean island," I said, as I always did. "Doesn't it?"

They looked at each other and frowned. I said, "Well, sort of? A little bit?"

My brother-in-law squinted at the pine trees, the grey water. "Well, yes," he said, anxious to please. "It *could* be. In a way." The Lucy Islands are twenty-four hundred miles further north, the water's colder by twenty degrees, and you can't pick coconuts off the beach. But on a sunny day, you can lie flat on hot sand and, if you close your eyes, almost hear the rumba band.

Fishing is very good on the shallows south of the islands, making the spot a popular destination for Prince Rupert residents. On weekends, there are sometimes large numbers of people picnicking on the beaches, but there's so much room that the Lucy

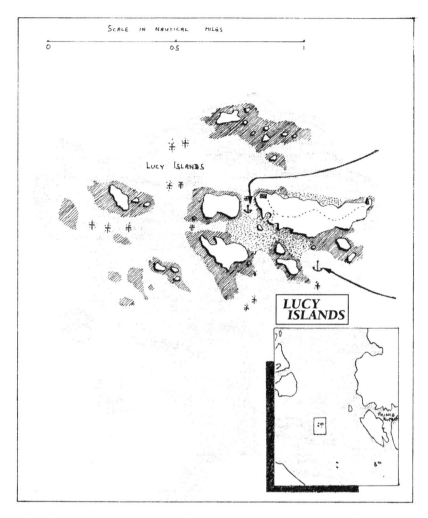

Islands are never crowded. And few people stay the night.

But an hour after sunset, the rhinoceros auklets come back to their burrows among the trees. Why these small seabirds time their arrival like that is a mystery, for the auklets have terrible eyesight. The first time we sat by a fire on the beach, we were startled to hear them whizzing past, like slow-moving artillery shells, fluttering down to crash land in the bushes behind us. We could hear them scurrying through the undergrowth toward their burrows, even twanging off the boat's rigging. But we never saw one of them, until we found a stuffed auklet at the Museum of Northern B.C. in Prince Rupert.

The Lucy Island lightstation was among the first left un-manned by Coast Guard automation. The supply ships used to

The Lucy Islands: not quite like a Caribbean atoll.

moor in the channel north of the main island, but the buoy has since been removed. A walking trail remains, leading from the helicopter pad on the western tip of the main island to the sad remains of the station on the eastern tip. A side trail leads to an outhouse above the southern beach of the main lagoon.

Day visitors often enter the lagoon west of the largest island. A rock sits right in the middle of the entrance, and northwesterly swells break on the point to the east. But once inside, the water is generally flat calm, though a heavy groundswell can roll through it in some conditions.

In our first boat, a tiny little cutter, we used to anchor quite securely in the lagoon. Even when the wind rose unexpectedly one night, and the waves of a southeaster came rolling right over the sandbars, we rode it out in there. I stayed up all night, drinking tea and reading Hornblower for inspiration, in case the anchor dragged. But it didn't. And our worst problem was landing the dinghy in the surf the next morning.

In our second boat we anchored once in the lagoon, and woke up at a forty-degree angle, hard aground on the falling tide. Deep-keeled boats should enter the lagoon with lots of water, and pay close attention to the depths; the bottom is clearly visible. We spent a couple of nights off the eastern tip of the main island, in a small bay to the south, frightfully exposed.

The auklets don't roost here, but big beetles come out at dusk and roam over the logs and rocks. They're gruesome-looking things, flat and hard-shelled. And tenacious. One somehow got in the dinghy with us one night, and ended up stretched out on the settee before either of us noticed.

Caution is needed for visiting the islands, not only for navigation among the numerous reefs and rocks, but also for changing weather. They are so exposed that they can quickly turn from pleasant to uncomfortable, and more quickly still to dangerous. But summer nights are frequently calm for a week or more at a stretch, and the Lucy Islands are truly beautiful.

49

DUNDAS ISLAND – EDITH HARBOUR

chart 3959/3991

D undas Island offers the last bit of shelter along the Canadian portion of the Inside Passage. Sitting on the edge of Dixon Entrance, its northern point is just six miles from Alaska.

Every year boats by the dozen pass Dundas and its chain of islands stretching south for sixteen miles. But few venture within the channels of this group, though it was once considered alongside South Moresby for status as a national park. With everything from swamps to sandy beaches, sheltered coves to wind-battered shores, the Dundas group forms one of the finest cruising grounds on the north coast, and one of the least visited anywhere on the Inside Passage. The only people who live here year-round are the lightkeepers of Green Island.

One of our favourite destinations is Edith Harbour, at the southwest tip of Dundas Island. A small number of mooring buoys are anchored here, specifically for the use of fishermen; a large trolling fleet works the west side of Dundas. But at high tide a cruising boat can slip north of the little islet at the harbour's northern end and anchor in a sheltered, empty lagoon. West of the harbour drying flats form a low-tide beach that connects to Prince Leboo Island. To the east the Dundas shore is peppered with small lakes filled with beaver dams. There doesn't seem to be much in the way of trout, but we did find a good catch of leeches.

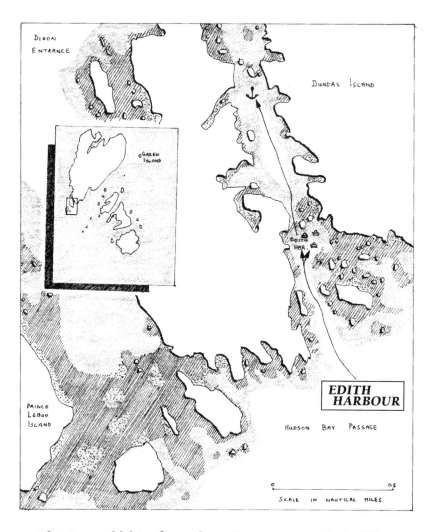

This is a wild bit of coastline. One stormy night in February of 1994, two fishboats ran aground on Prince Leboo. A small gillnetter sits high on the beach, its hull and wheelhouse pierced by driftwood logs. Southeasters require special caution, even in the summer. We spent one of the most uncomfortable nights we've ever had anchored on the rocky west shore of Dundas, while waves eight feet high swept up Caamaño Passage.

The harbour mouth is open to the south, so arrival should be postponed during bouts of bad weather. In addition:

~ The gap leading from the harbour to the lagoon dries at low tide. Entrance is best at high slack.

~ It's half a mile across the drying flats to Prince Leboo. The ground is uneven in places, and walking over it requires some effort. The tide has to be watched *very carefully* as it comes up quickly. The three outer islands are Native Reserves.

~ The bush can be quite thick on the island at Edith Harbour's west side. We took two compasses for a quarter-mile hike across to the outer shore, and still came back well off course.

~ The beaver lakes east of the cove look pleasant for swimming. But watch for the leeches.

~ The entire Dundas group is haunted by a reputation as the bug capital of Canada. Fishermen say the insects are so bad that seine boats carry mosquito netting for the beach man. We've never had much of a problem, but others have cut short trips to Dundas when horse-flies started nibbling at the mosquito bites. Take a good stock of bug repellant, and a swath of net to drape over the hatches.

≈ 50 ≈
DUNDAS ISLAND – BRUNDIGE INLET

chart 3960/3991

The north coast of Dundas Island beyond the Green Island lightstation is indented by three bays. Brundige Inlet, in the centre, is the one most often recommended to cruisers crossing Dixon Entrance. Goose Bay, to the west, is used by fishermen trolling off the island's tip. To the east is an unnamed bay, the shallowest of the three, and our particular favourite.

The entrance is easy: keep well north of the outlying inlets, and approach the bay from the west. A basin of eight or nine fathoms opens below the southern tip of the skinny island within the bay. Watch for the drying flat at the head, and anchor anywhere within the basin. Sports fishermen sometimes drop crab traps on the edge of the shallows.

Anchored here, you can look north past the Gnarled Islands to the mountains of Alaska. The border is less than five miles away.

In some conditions, Brundige Inlet may offer better shelter for small boats. Chart 3909 – replacing older chart 3980 – is a detailed plan of the inlet and its popular anchorage.

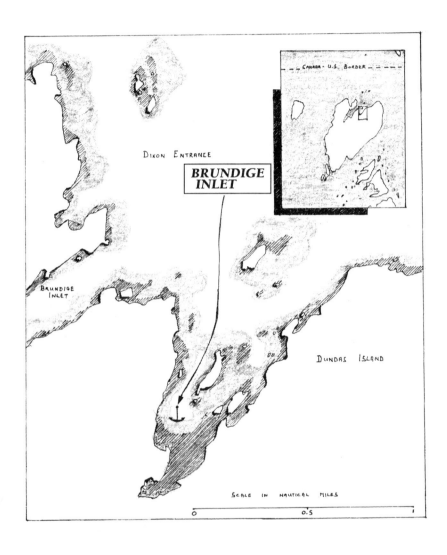

DIXON ENTRANCE

BRUNDIGE INLET

CANADA - U.S. BORDER

BRUNDIGE INLET

DUNDAS ISLAND

SCALE IN NAUTICAL MILES

0   0.5   1

≈ THE CHARTED LIBERTINE ≈

We live in Prince Rupert on a hill above the harbour. Each spring we see the first cruisers returning to the port after a winter away. As the weather warms, they come in greater and greater numbers—some alone and some in little groups. They settle along the wharves, resting there. And on the first clear morning they're gone again, moving north. But others take their place, following the same ancient route, resting in the same places. It's a wonderful thing to see, amazing really. You can't help but wonder: How do they find their way?

We've met some boaters who navigate on table placemats, on road maps and aerial photographs. We even met one who had no maps at all, not even a postcard. He was just following the other boats all the way from Seattle to Alaska, turning left or right according to the guy ahead.

In early summer he followed them into Prince Rupert Harbour like a cow to a barn, and came knocking on our door, to ask for directions. He had no compass, other than the tiny thing built into his binoculars, no reference books, and the woman with him had never set foot on a boat before she signed aboard in Puget Sound. All he wanted was to be pointed again in the right direction. But he'd already made it all the way to Prince Rupert, and even though his boat did dry up on the mud below our house, I'm sure he got it off and arrived safely in Alaska. God looks after people like that.

And the Canadian Hydrographic Service looks after everyone else.

As well as updating the marine charts, the Hydrographic Service publishes an annual edition of the *Sailing Directions*, describing in

minute detail every inch of the B.C. coast. Our copy is several years old, the cover faded by the sun, many pages splattered by rough-weather spills of coffee and tea. With the *Pilot*—the colloquial name for all volumes of *Sailing Directions*—and the proper charts, the small-boat navigator can go anywhere he likes.

I think we carry more charts than most people. We take about fifty just for the distance between Prince Rupert and Port Hardy. We have another packet under the dog's berth in case we venture south of there, a few more in with the lentils and kidney beans on the chance that we might find ourselves, somehow, over on the Charlottes.

But still we have a few gaps on the outer coast that we hope to fill in this year, or maybe next. And if we ever headed up the long channels—Douglas and Gardner or Fisher and Dean, we'd find ourselves very quickly in uncharted waters.

We keep our regular stock of fifty arranged by number, standing upright in a three-sided bin against the frames. From these we pick out the two or three in our general area and keep them folded in a plastic envelope that's not quite as waterproof as it's supposed to be. We keep that in the cockpit, and we use it often.

When Kristin's steering, she keeps her finger on the chart and shunts it along with the progress of the boat. She likes to know exactly where she is at every moment. It infuriates her to come up from below, ask me where we are, see me sketch a huge circle on the plastic and hear me say, "Somewhere in here." She snatches it up, orients it to the landscape. And she starts pointing. "Okay. That island over there must be this one. Right? Right?!"

In Lama Passage we responded once to a red smoke flare. We could see the boat, two miles or so ahead, and we called him on the radio to let him know we'd spotted his signal.

"Calling the vessel off Serpent Point," I said into the microphone. There was no response. "The vessel off Serpent Point.

The vessel lighting smoke flares?"

I shrugged, and turned off the radio. When we got up to the boat—a little outboard cruiser—we saw three people lounging like seals on the deck and cabin top. Right away, one of them jumped up and locked the cabin door. Then someone else came to the rail and caught a line.

"We heard you calling us," he said. "But we didn't know where the hell Serpent Point was."

So we use the real charts. And we keep close track of where we are.

It's amazing how many people travel along the coast with nothing more than the *Marine Atlas* as a guide. It shows the courses for them, the distances, even an anchorage here and there. Well, we have one on our boat. And I wouldn't want to be without it. It's helpful for getting a look at things on a broad scale, or for use as a notebook to record favourite places. But it's always with a bit of embarrassment that I drag it out. As soon as Kristin sees it, she rolls her eyes.

"We're not using *that* thing, are we?" she says.

"Just a look," I say.

The problem is, it's not always accurate and a lot of the information is not kept up to date. I often wonder how many cruisers avoid the wide, open waters of Lewis Passage because the *Atlas* says it's dangerous. How many went looking for a fuel barge in Butedale during the decade that there wasn't one to be found? Probably fewer thread their way up the Skeena River to the flattened ruins of Port Essington where, the *Marine Atlas* says, a store and fuel can be found in the summer.

But worse of all, the land isn't always where it's supposed to be. Use the *Marine Atlas* to find your way into some places and you'll know how Captain Ahab felt aboard the old *Pequod*. You'll find land where there is no land.

One night, stuck for an anchorage in the gathering dark, we used the *Atlas* to find our way into a bay in the Estevan Group. It looked okay, free of dangers, and we just steered in a zigzag through the huge rafts of kelp. We put down the anchors in a clear spot, and went to sleep. In the morning, at low tide, we found ourselves ringed in by jagged, vicious rocks, like a minnow trapped in a shark's mouth. If we'd anchored a few feet to the left, a few feet to the right, it wouldn't have seemed nearly so amusing.

The *Atlas* carries a warning on every page that the maps are for reference only. This was why.

Sure, real charts are expensive. But so are shipyard bills. And you don't need that many, not really. Used charts are available at second-hand places like The Sailor's Exchange or Popeye's in Sidney. If you're happy moving along the freeway, from Horsefly Cove to Butedale to Lowe Inlet, the *Atlas* might get you there. But once you take the first exit, you'll want the Canadian Hydrographic Service charts close at hand. And a red pen to write "METRIC!" in a dozen places across the new ones. There's nothing like the feeling of finding out that depths are really half of what you think the chart is telling you.

It's one of the reasons that I envy the Little People, the kayakers and the rowers. They can quite happily get along with the small-scale charts covering vast distances. Some even find that topographical maps are more useful than marine charts, as they're more likely to show good spots for camping. But for the boat that draws four or five feet trying to find its way into a labyrinth anchorage, nothing can take the place of a marine chart that shows the rocks as little stars. And someone standing on the bow.

Because we so often go south while everyone else is going north, people sometimes ask us what's ahead for them. One couple, on a big cement sailboat, asked if we'd show them some anchorages around Prince Rupert. The man went below, and fetched up his charts.

He spread them open on the cockpit coaming. We bent closer; we hadn't seen many charts in black and white. I showed him the way into Dodge Cove.

"There should be a light here," I said. It wasn't on the chart. There weren't any lights on the chart.

Kristin frowned. "When was this made?" she said. She took off her glasses and peered at the little box with all the printing on it. "Nineteen twenty-three? Where did you get this? An antique shop?" Yes. That was exactly where they'd got it. They were finding their way around quite happily, quite safely, with information sixty years old. And I guess there's a lesson there too. All the charts in the world aren't much help without good seamanship to back them up.

Or good luck.

≈ SEAT-OF-THE-PANTS PILOTAGE ≈

When English yachtsman and writer Peter Pye sailed through the northern coast in the mid-1950s, huge sections of his charts were marked "unexamined." Even Kwakshua Channel was just a crude sketch on his small-scale charts. His boat was an old cutter named *Moonraker*—"A ship that looks like a box and sails like a witch," he wrote. But he took her through those unplumbed passages without any of the modern conveniences, including an engine.

He did it, he said, by keeping one hand in God's pocket, very tightly clenched.

Doctor Pye didn't need a radar set or forward-scanning sonar; he'd never heard of loran or satellite navigation. He towed a twirling log behind his boat to gauge distance and speed, and, when he had to, he scrambled up to the cross-trees for a glance around.

"Looking back on the short time we spent on that bit of coast," he wrote in his book *The Sea is for Sailing*, "I can't remember anything I've enjoyed more. 'Local knowledge is essential,' is how the *Pilot* would describe some of the places we poked our noses into, and I must admit there were times when a little would have come in handy."

Today, less than fifty years later, the *Pilot* still carries the same warnings. Though the charts are infinitely improved, there are still places unsounded, shores drawn in squiggly lines. And the small-boat navigator, with or without an array of electronic machinery, is sometimes not much better off than the crew of *Moonraker*. When it comes to radar and loran, local knowledge—like batteries—is not included.

"In time," said Doctor Pye, "we acquired some sort of local knowledge ourselves." And that is still the best way to do it.

The first time we set off down the Inside Passage, we had nothing in the way of electronics except for one cabin light and a VHF radio, both powered by a big eight-cell battery discarded from a city bus. We didn't even have an alternator; we just recharged the battery at Port Hardy and kept on going.

We longed for loran as we slogged across Queen Charlotte Sound in a rising southeaster, the visibility less than half a mile. We wished we had a radar set when the fog came down on us in the straits, and we couldn't tell if the shapes ahead were rocks or boats.

The second year I said enough was enough, and I bought a depth sounder. It was the flasher type, with a light that went round and round as we neared the shore, flickering like the leaping ball in a roulette wheel. And if we looked away even once as it hovered around the zero mark, we were never sure if there was still a hundred feet of water under the keel, or nothing at all. Instead of solving our problems, it only added to them.

When in doubt we still got out the lead sinker and the bit of string. I remember leaning over the side with the boat anchored close to the head of a little bay. Kristin was standing behind me, peering over my shoulder, as I let the string unwind from its dowel. "Is it deep enough?" she said.

The string was just fifteen feet long. It jumped off the dowel in Slinky coils and snaked between my fingers. Kristin made a little noise as the end peeled off the wood, flicked through my hand, and sank down under the boat.

"I guess it's deep enough," I said.

Two years later Kristin's boat-building brother got us a second-hand loran at a bargain price. I spent days playing with it at the dock, setting the drift alarm at miniscule amounts just to hear it go off as the boat tugged at the mooring lines. But the first time we used it, it put us half a mile off course as we searched for one tiny bay in a shoreline riddled with inlets and coves. And out came the hand-bearing compass again, and the brass dividers.

The loran was a mixed blessing. I found I could spend half an hour punching in waypoints, or do the same thing in ten minutes with a pencil and a parallel rule. But the machine made a wonderful steering compass on thick, overcast days. It would show us our speed to the tenth of a knot, our exact course with the effects of current and wind. It took us across Hakai Passage in zero visibility, while the currents swirled in every direction. I hunched over the machine, chanting course headings as they flashed on the screen. My brother steered left, then right, as we bobbed on a big ocean swell. We heard the surf ahead, saw nothing at all until the narrow passage opened in the fog right where it should have been. And that day I wouldn't have traded the loran for anything.

So I put on an alternator, and our motoring speed dropped by a knot, because of the drag on the little eight-horse diesel.

For every silver lining, there's a cloud.

Electronics are a luxury, not a necessity. It's a good feeling to find your own way along a stretch of coastline, to head out into the fog and drizzle with only your compass and end up exactly where you're going. Whether it's one tiny light buoy three miles away, or a whole shore thirty miles across the Sound, seeing your destination materialize off the bow gives you a wonderful confidence you'd never earn with black boxes and flickering screens.

It's a big step heading out that first time into a thick fog or a moonless night. When we made our first night passage under sail, Kristin pottered around the boat filling thermoses and arranging charts as the sun set, huge and red. Then she pushed open the hatch and looked up at the sky. "It's time for that dog to go below," she said. "It's going to be dark very, very soon."

The Skipper didn't want to go. She growled and snapped as Kristin packed her down. And in a moment, they were both back on deck.

"There's still lots of time," said Kristin. "I forgot I had my sunglasses on."

We sailed all that night with the mainsail reefed down and the staysail furled. Black waves burst on the bow and tossed up filmy spray; gulls rose like pale ghosts as we woke them sleeping in the troughs. And the masthead made long, lazy spirals across the stars.

At dawn we shook out the reefs and kept on going. We'd travelled thirty miles from dark to light, steering just by the wind and the waves, and we'd arrived into a whole new realm of cruising.

With no proper table in little *Nid*, we do our chart work in the cockpit or on the broad counter just inside the companionway. For the most part, it's quick and dirty.

Usually, it's enough to gauge our position by lining up natural range markers: a prominent point first appearing round the bulge of coast; an islet eclipsing another behind it. We've laid everything from filleting knives to gaff handles on the chart, connecting the landmarks to determine our position based on our distance from shore. It takes just a few seconds, and it's close enough for most purposes.

Often, we just press the chart flat on the cockpit and roll a pencil over its plastic cover to give us a crude bearing on the compass rose, then lay the pencil along the latitudes to measure distance. And we don't bother with the fancy stuff; we use the inner circle on the rose, and ignore both true north and variation. Even on our oldest charts, the ones that have celebrated their twentieth birthday, the three-minute-a-year change in variation adds an error of only one degree to our bearings.

We've found that an easy way to orient ourselves to a confusing coastline is to look at the chart at a shallow angle, along its plane, as though sighting down an orienteering compass; the landscape seems to leap out, almost in 3D.

But for careful work, we use a hand-bearing compass. Marking the bearings of two prominent points puts us pretty close to the intersection; with three we can be as exact as any loran. And in a sort of reverse method, we can draw a line on a chart and use the compass to know when we've crossed it.

We used that method to give a wide berth to the reefs and islets around McInnes Island as the night darkened. We knew our course was taking us well outside the islands, but we had to be careful not to turn too soon. By extending a line through

McInnes Island to the tip of Price Island, we knew we could keep going on our original course until the bearing on the compass matched the line. It was unnerving; rocks are scattered far out, like spilled salt, and we'd seen great plumes of spray from miles off. But the one bearing kept us free of all dangers.

But the hand-bearing compass is most useful for approaching unfamiliar anchorages. With it we can stay well off the shore until the correct bearing on a point inside the bay lets us turn in for a clear run through the outlying hazards. From there, it's usually a simple matter to find natural range marks that lead us deeper into the anchorage.

These range marks are also useful for determining drift due to wind or current. If the land directly ahead seems to move sideways, we are being carried off course. The simplest solution is to adjust the boat's heading until the range markers stay in line. We won't be aiming where we want to go; we'll be crabbing sideways through the water, but taking the shortest path to get there.

Where the shore is too distant to make out natural range marks, drift becomes obvious when we're constantly adjusting course to head for the same landmark. We could keep going like that, approaching the shore in a long, sweeping curve, but it's often preferable to head the boat slightly into the wind or current and, using the steering compass, close the shore at an angle. In poor visibility, it's the only way to do it.

There comes a time when this seat-of-the-pants pilotage becomes second nature. We find ourselves always keeping track of our position through one means or another, though only rarely marking it on a chart. I was surprised to find that my brother, an avid kayaker, used the same techniques himself—right down to letting his pencil do double duty as ruler and dividers. But it made sense; a kayaker has to navigate not only with no instruments, but with no hands. And through him I found one of the best books on pilotage I've ever seen: David Burch's *Fundamentals of Kayak Navigation*. With a straight-forward text and simple illustrations, Mr. Burch outlines a method of pilotage perfect for any small-boat navigator.

Electronic gadgets, though wonderful luxuries, are not essential for safe coastal cruising. Especially for the typical cruiser operated by two people, some form of self-steering would be a wiser purchase than either loran or radar. That's my next priority. All I ask is a tall ship, and an autopilot to steer her by.

≈ ANCHORS AND ANCHORING ≈

Nid's main anchor is a sort of modified Danforth, like the kind hanging from the bow chocks of just about every fishboat on the coast. It weighs thirty-five pounds, backed up by fifty feet of three-eighth inch chain shackled to twenty-five fathoms of five-eighth-inch nylon rode and twenty fathoms of three-quarter-inch. It's a bit of work sometimes to haul it up by hand, but still it's barely enough.

The usual advice suggests that a boat can anchor safely in a depth no more than a quarter of the length of its chain and line. For *Nid*, that would limit us to places not more than eighty feet deep at high tide. And the rule applies only in fair weather.

But lashed to a bracket on the boat's stern is another anchor, the typical flat, triangular spade that most small pleasure boats use. It holds like a bloodsucker in sand or mud, but is almost useless in rock, or on any bottom thick with weeds. It's shackled to four feet of half-inch chain, and thirty-four fathoms of three-eighth-inch nylon.

Every night I set both anchors.

I learned my lesson one night in Klemtu Passage. We just had the one anchor down, and the boat was swinging with the tide, back and forth: three changes between the time we anchored and the time we left the next day.

When I hauled on the line, it went immediately taut. One pull, and the whole thing came up from the bottom, all the chain and a huge chunk of rope snarled hopelessly around the flukes. If we'd waited another couple of hours, it would have picked itself up just from the rising of the tide.

The next night, and every one since, I've set the main anchor and then rowed out in the dinghy with the little spade anchor. Sometimes I drop it off the stern to stop the boat from swinging altogether, but usually both anchor lines feed through the same bow chock and *Nid* will snub up on one and then the other. The more windy it is, the closer together I put the anchors, and the greater the scope the better. At an angle of thirty degrees, the holding power of each anchor is doubled. And that way we've sat through full gales with both lines humming taut, and never moved an inch.

If we are close to shore, we sometimes use a floating polypropylene line instead of the stern anchor, and tie it to a convenient tree. We tie the boat fenders at intervals along its length so others will be sure to see it.

In places where the tide runs heavily and we're not sure the anchors will get a good bite on the bottom, or when the wind is likely to veer and rise, we put out the two anchors and take another line to shore. And *Nid* sits in the middle, like a spider in its web, swinging slowly round. The lines wrap across each other, but it's a simple matter to untwist them from the deck on each change of the tide.

For extra security we carry a few twenty-pound lead cannonballs. They hang from large shackles spliced to thirty-foot lengths of plastic rope. Lowering one of them on the rode keeps the force on the anchor more horizontal, and increases the holding power by a huge degree. Some boaters accomplish the same thing by tying fenders or floats to the rode, but we prefer the weights.

We're usually anchored alone in little bays and isolated nooks. But in places where other boats gather, our cautious anchoring means we end up taking more than our share of space because

Nid won't swing with the rest of the fleet. Though we try to stay off at the edges of the anchorage, I've been yelled at by a loud American who stood screaming on his flying bridge. And I've inconvenienced others who only reacted more politely.

But I've always slept well. And there's lots of room on the north coast.

Anchors are the best insurance you could ever buy.

≈ COASTAL COMMUNITIES ≈

T here's no fuel at Hartley Bay," the boaters told us. They got up from their deck chairs and leaned over the rail of the little aft deck. Water gurgled from the exhaust of a big generator and pushed at the dinghy. I paddled with the oars; I didn't want to rub against the boat, smudging Avon-black on a hull as huge and white as Tom Sawyer's picket fence.

"Is there a store?" I said.

"What do you need?" he said. It sounded as though—whatever it was—he'd hand it down by the bushel.

"Just some vegetables," I said. "Onions and potatoes."

"Hmm," he said. "You might find that. I'm sure there's something there."

Hartley Bay wasn't that far out of the way. The very next day we slipped past the breakwater and into the harbour. On shore a group of children scrambled along the rocks in orange lifejackets, the drawstrings flapping at their feet. Before we'd tied the docklines, a young man was standing beside us.

"Do you want to buy Indian art?" he said. "I do art. Like this."

He put his foot up on the dock rail. Across his thigh, in ballpoint pen, he'd drawn an elaborate eagle on the worn denim.

"We don't have much money," Kristin said, and his head dropped a bit. "But it's good. That's really good."

He smiled. "Is the coffee pot on?"

He sat with us in *Nid*'s little cockpit, his arm draped over the tiller, and drank black tea. Then he asked for a pencil, and a bit of paper, and he drew us an eagle and a raven and a killer whale. On the breakwater the children shrieked excitedly.

He looked up, then down again. "The otters have babies," he said.

"Is there a store here?" said Kristin.

"Sure there's a store," he said. "I'll show you."

"But no fuel?" I said.

He frowned. "It's not here now. It's usually tied up there." He pointed toward the dockhead. "But it's not here now."

I told him what the boaters had said. His finger traced along the eagle on his jeans. "Those were the proud people," he said.

He took Kristin through the village to the little store in the basement of somebody's house. And he carried back the box of good potatoes, fist-sized onions and fresh oranges. He untied the docklines and watched us go, then thrust his hands in his pockets, and the eagle on his pants stretched its wings.

"See you," he said, and turned away.

There are several small communities scattered through the 245 miles between Cape Caution and Prince Rupert. Bella Bella and Klemtu both have fully equipped fuel docks and small grocery stores. Namu has had both, but probably shouldn't be relied on. Shearwater has a shipyard and post office, but no stores. In Kitkatla, like Hartley Bay, day-to-day needs are available from home businesses run privately for the convenience of village residents.

Port Edward has a good marine supply-and-service centre, but other stores are a considerable distance from the water.

Prince Rupert is a city of sixteen thousand, home port of the largest fishing fleet on the northern coast. Wharfingers prefer transient boats to use the Rushbrook floats at the east end of the city. You'll usually have to raft up; always in fishing season. It means a fairly long walk, or a taxi ride, but the larger chain stores will deliver groceries to the docks. Cow Bay, next to the Prince Rupert Yacht and Rowing Club, is more convenient, but very small. It is often so crowded that even the logboom is lined with fishboats. But showers are a few blocks away at Pioneer Rooms.

Port Simpson is a fine harbour north of Prince Rupert. It's a major gathering place for the herring fleet, a place busy with floatplanes and deep-sea log ships. The village, called Lax Kw'Alaams, is on the site of a Hudson's Bay Company trading post established in 1834. There is a small store, a cafe and a post office. A large cannery is located on the spit at the west side of the harbour, just above the small-craft docks.

Bella Bella, midway up the coast, is the busiest of the small coastal communities. The B.C. Ferries stop here once a week northbound, once a week southbound, but there are no facilities for loading or unloading vehicles. All freight for the village is carried by hand through the ferry's side door and down a metal gangway. For the Little People it's particularly inconvenient. Kayaks are sometimes launched or loaded through the side door, sometimes off the car deck. When the *Queen of the North*'s bow visor was welded shut in the fall of 1994, all kayaks were carted through the side door and between the pink-covered tables in the cafeteria. But by then plans were already underway to construct a proper ferry dock in McLoughlin Bay, just to the south of Bella Bella.

More properly called Waglisla, the village has a post office and hotel, good food and liquor stores, and several small businesses operated from private homes, including a bakery and a video rental outlet. The Canadian Imperial Bank of Commerce has a branch office in Waglisla open two or three days a week. There is also a small hospital and dental office, and showers at the hotel.

Because of its central location, the community is the major refueling stop for both commercial and pleasure fleets. It is one of the few places where kerosene is available by bulk. Larger craft—the seiners and Coast Guard boats—tie up to the outside of the ferry wharf, but all others jostle for room along a few feet of dock inside the main wharf.

At times small boats may have quite a wait to get in next to the fuel hoses. We often tie up to the mooring buoys north of the dock and row back with jerry cans. But most people wait, and some just muscle in. But it's not advisable to fuel up and then leave your boat at the dock while you visit the food and liquor stores; we saw a fisherman untie a sailboat's stern line and let the boat drift so he could work in at its place.

≈ WEATHER WISE ≈

We came up Queens Sound and met the rain just south of Superstition Point. It was the sort of rain that hammers the sea into a flat, steely sheet, where ball-bearing drops stand on the surface like rivets. It came down through our collars and up through our pants, and it turned our fingers to white, pulpy worms.

The sky closed in around us, hiding first the sun, then everything else, behind a white curtain of falling water. I had to squint into the pale glow at the changing shapes, as though travelling snowblind like Scott through an empty Antarctica, a land of white. And when we anchored, it seemed to be right at the centre of that world. And there ahead of us, like Amundsen, was a group of Little People camped on the beach.

We went below, shed sou'westers and rain pants, slickers and capes. And we put a pot on the cabin floor, and watched it fill through a leak in a deck prism.

By morning the rain had eased to drizzle and fog. We rowed to the beach to say hello, and found the kayakers busy with a breakfast of coffee and pancake mix. They weren't very happy Little People; they weren't even very little Little People. Three big, husky men; I couldn't imagine how they squeezed themselves into their narrow boats.

They'd come from Vancouver, hoping to find solitude and adventure, like the canoeists in the movie *Deliverance*. But there were too many people, they said, and it rained too much, and the scenery was pretty dismal. They were just passing time until their charter boat came to pick them up and take them back to civilization.

"We were hoping to get to the Goose Islands," one of them told us. "But I don't think we'll bother. One wet, rainy beach is pretty much like the next one."

We left them there, headed out ourselves into the fog. And just a mile away, the skies cleared to icy blue and a huge, swollen sun burned the water into steam. We didn't see rain for another three days until we arrived in Bella Bella under skies quilted with clouds. And there at the dock were the same three Little People, their kayaks stuffed into a small powerboat like furled umbrellas wedged in a stand.

I asked if they'd made it out to the Goose Islands.

"Yeah, we did," they said. "But there was nowhere to walk. There was nothing to do."

We got fuel and groceries, then continued on our way. And again, just a mile away, the sky was sunny and clear. It was as though the rain followed those kayakers, tracked them from place to place. And wherever they went, the scenery really would be dismal, the beaches all the same.

But it's a fact of life on the north coast. If you go cruising beyond Cape Caution, you have to accept the fact that it's going to rain.

Prince Rupert is the same distance north of the equator as Tierra Del Fuego is to the south. If it was in the southern hemisphere, the city would be just a hundred miles short of Cape Horn. In both places, the latitudes are high, and the weather fierce. Along the B.C. coast, says the *Sailing Directions*, "winds in excess of sixty-five knots have been recorded in exposed areas, and it is estimated that gusts up to one hundred knots do occur." Yachtsman Peter Pye, in his book *The Sea is for Sailing*, wrote that parts of the northern coast have been compared to the landscapes of the Magellan Straits. He quoted an old expression: "Men sail the seven seas *and* the Hecate Strait."

Fortunately, the worst of the weather comes in winter, when southeast gales drive in like freight trains, thundering through one after another. But even in July, southerly winds of force eight have been recorded in Chatham Sound, force nine off Cape St. James. You can feel them coming for days, these big summer storms.

Fair-weather winds blow from the west and northwest. Typically, they rise from a morning calm to force three or four, and then ease off again in the evening. When a high-pressure ridge stabilizes off the coast, the pattern can stay like that for weeks. The days will be warm and sunny, the afternoons windy and the nights clear, but the price will be fog in the mornings, thick banks of it that fill in from the sea.

If the high-pressure ridge moves inshore, or fails to develop, summer weather is cold and wet. The wind shifts to the south-east and low clouds weep over land and sea. And *that* pattern holds forever. For sailboats steered from open cockpits, it's miserable. For the Little People in their open boats, it must be almost unendurable.

The journals of Captain Vancouver are filled with references to inclement and melancholy weather. He wrote of tents flooding in the rain, of crews fearful that summer gales would sweep away their boats and leave them marooned forever on a shore Vancouver called inhospitable, "whose solitary and desolate appearance, though daily more familiarized to our view, did not become less irksome to our feelings." The weather was so bad in the summers of 1792 and 1793 that he had awnings erected over the open boats, and issued an additional quantity of spirits to their crews, "a practice that was found to be necessary to be continued throughout the season."

Two hundred years later, summers on the northern coast are sometimes just the same, sometimes just the opposite. But the trend seems to be toward longer periods of good weather, hot and sunny. Kristin says it's global warming; I think it's the El Niño.

But the end result is that sunscreen and tinted glasses, shorts and cotton shirts have to be packed side by side with wool sweaters and foul-weather gear. Boaters spending more than a few days on the northern coast should be ready for everything from cold rain to blistering sun.

The weather is not only changeable but unpredictable; even the Coast Guard Radio broadcasts often miss the mark. One year we were anchored in Seaforth Channel on our way south, listening as every broadcast predicted an imminent end to the rain and a change to northerly winds. It was infuriating; we could see for ourselves that no change was coming. But the forecasts went on and on, and every melancholy morning was another disappointment. After a few days a big U.S. cutter came into our anchorage, a husband and wife. We started talking, and he mentioned that he was going to write to the Canadian weather service after his voyage.

"I've been thinking that too," I said. "They're wrong. They're always wrong."

He looked at me. "I think they do a wonderful job," he said. And in the morning, he raised his sails and continued on his way. To the north.

The Coast Guard Radio operators broadcast from windowless

rooms, reading reports prepared in Vancouver. Though the northern coast is broken into several forecast areas, each one is huge, and conditions can vary greatly from place to place within them. Northwesterly winds on the outer coast can become southeasters when they start winding through the coastal inlets. Don't sit in the sunshine at Namu and wait for southerly winds to change; it's probably blowing from the northwest in Queen Charlotte Sound.

Mariners soon learn to accept the forecasts as a guide and to listen more carefully to the reports from lightstations and automated buoys. The reports are updated more frequently than the live broadcasts, and they give actual conditions of wind and sea and barometric pressure at specific sites up and down the coast. It was this network of reporting stations that impressed the U.S. sailor so much that he would write a thank-you note to Environment Canada.

The agency publishes a booklet that helps the boater interpret weather data. Available at most places where charts are sold, it's a useful tool to have on board, especially as efforts continue towards an eventual replacement of lightkeepers with machines. Weather information from the lightstations is not included in live broadcasts and, except when rare "bulletins" are issued, can be as much as four hours old.

"What do you think the wind speed is?" asked Kristin, as we sailed past McInnes Island in a boisterous westerly. It had been building all morning, the waves stacking one atop another until they sloshed occasionally over the foredeck.

I guessed it was about fifteen knots. We had a reef in the main as we ploughed a weaving furrow past the lighthouse and on into the open sea. But when we turned on the radio, we got a bit of a surprise. The wind, it said, was just three knots.

"No way," said Kristin.

I said, "A machine could do better than that," which was probably exactly what I was supposed to think. But the report was hours old, issued during the morning calms.

"Three knots?" said Kristin. A wave broke against the hull, and she ducked in the spray. "I'd hate to be out here if it ever got up to five."

≈ WATER, WATER, EVERYWHERE ≈

Nid has no built-in water tank. We carry about twelve gallons in portable, plastic drums, and refill them wherever we can. Usually it's just a tiny creek that empties straight into the sea over a jumble of rocks. We anchor off the mouth and carry our drums above the tide line. The water is often stained yellow by its passage through muskeg, but it tastes better than anything out of a tap.

The creeks shown on the charts usually provide water all summer. But many others aren't shown, and after a heavy rain just about any nook or cove has fresh water gushing from its head.

We never worried about Giardia—or beaver fever—before we met a pair of kayakers on the other inside passage. They'd picked up the parasite in a remote creek halfway up the coast, and one of them had been flat on his back for a week before he could paddle again. "At least ours is the only type of engine," he said, "that heals itself just by resting."

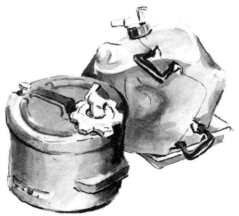

It's a sad fact that just about every river, stream or trickle of water may carry Giardia. If there's a good flow in the creek, we still drink the water just as it comes out of the ground. We probably shouldn't, but we do. But wherever it's flat, and slow-moving, we boil every bit before we drink it.

Some sources say water must be boiled for five minutes or more to kill the Giardia and other micro-organisms. Others say bringing it to the boiling point is enough, and that's the advice we've followed, with no ill effects in the last six years. Filters and chemical treatments are available in outdoor stores, but we've found boiling to be the simplest solution.

≈ COOKING AFLOAT AND ASHORE ≈

Our first boat stove was a one-burner butane model fueled by eight-ounce cylinders. It was dependable and efficient, but expensive to operate. And using the stove in a closed cabin gave us fierce headaches.

Soon we moved up to a two-burner alcohol stove of the unpressurised absorption type. Each burner had a separate cannister packed with wicking. We had to refill them through a tiny funnel, but once full they burned for hours. We used methyl hydrate, bought in five-gallon jugs, and burned—or evaporated—more than a gallon a week. It was easy to light, though singed fingers were a common hazard, but as hard to extinguish as a forest fire. There were none of the baffles that the modern stoves have; we jammed a cork down through the mouth of each canister. The stove worked well, until we refilled the canisters with shellac thinner by mistake.

And then we moved up again, to a diesel stove. It's a two-burner model, with a brass tank built into a stainless-steel body. The burners have to be pre-heated by burning methyl hydrate in little open cups; if the boat's heeled, this is very hard to do. We had our first boat fire when methyl hydrate slopped out of the cups and leaked round the failed welds onto the counter below the stove. Like alcohol, methyl hydrate is invisible when it burns, so we didn't discover the fire until the wood scorched and a plastic mug was set aflame.

And our next stove will be propane.

For years we thought it too dangerous to cook with explosive fuel. But after dabbling with the alternatives, we're ready to take what small risk remains when all the precautions are taken. We'll have the tank outside and sniffers inside, and a positive, electronic shut-off in case we forget to close the valve. And for the first time ever, we'll be cooking with gas.

Baking

Even on our open, two-burner stove we cook cakes and scones and yeast-risen bread thanks to a little portable oven that Kristin found through Mountain Equipment Co-op in Vancouver. Designed for back-packers, the Outback Oven breaks down into a package the size of a pie plate. In use it balances on a wire frame above a circular heat-spreader, the whole thing contained in a sort of foil-cloth hood. We've used it under way, with springs and hooks to lash it down, but it works best at anchor, when we can wrestle with the stove to get the low, steady flame the oven requires.

The Outback Oven is one of the few things on the boat that works better than we'd hoped, year after year.

Barbecuing

It's one of our greatest pleasures to go ashore with a freshly caught salmon for a barbecue on the beach. We take a wire rack coated in some sort of ceramic; it never rusts and it scrubs clean with a handful of seaweed.

Even after a week of rain there's plenty of half-dry wood among the roots of shoreside trees. Little knots of pine sap and twig-ends bearded with moss start any fire going. The chunks of evergreen bark that litter every beach burn like charcoal briquettes, and break down into coals perfect for baking potatoes. It's a lucky day when we're on a sandy beach. When the fire's down to coals, we scrape it aside and bury the potatoes in the hot oven underneath, then rebuild the fire on top. Among rocks, we just chuck them into the coals and take our chances. "I like them a little black," says Kristin, when they come out hard as stones.

The fish goes on the grill in thick fillets, skin side up until the flesh turns slightly brown. Then we flip the slabs over, drench them with melted butter and crushed garlic. It's done when the flesh separates from the skin and flakes apart at the touch of a fork.

Salads

For the last few years, Kristin has been growing bean sprouts on the boat. She puts raw mung beans, alfafa seeds or lentils, into a mason jar and soaks them overnight in fresh water. Then she drains them and rinses them several times a day with small amounts of fresh water. The jars are sealed with bits of mesh in place of the glass lids, and left to drain upside down after each bath. If kept in the sun, the sprouts are ready to eat in three days. Mixed with canned corn, a bit of vinegar and oil, they make a delicious salad.

"It's amazing," I told her. "Like a little farm."

"What?" she said. "Most people wouldn't call it amazing."

Laurel's Kitchen, though not one of Kristin's favourite cookbooks, says, "When a seed sprouts, its food value skyrockets. Vitamin C materializes as if by magic, and other nutrients increase several times over." It recommends working with a tablespoon of seeds or a third of a cup of beans, and adds to Kristin's meager list garbanzos, peas and wheat berries. Anything that hasn't sprouted in three days, says *Laurel's Kitchen*, isn't going to grow at all.

Jams

Kristin also makes jam from the plentiful huckleberries of the north coast, using a big kettle on the kerosene stove. It seems a painless process, but I don't stay around to watch. The scraping of her spoon on the pot bottom sets my teeth tingling; it makes me shiver and jump.

Once I snapped at her: "Can't you use a spatula?".

She kept stirring. "Oh, I could," she said patiently, "if you don't mind bits of plastic in your jam."

Kristin uses standard canning jars and their screw-on lids rather than relying on a paraffin seal that might not stand up to stormy weather. Whatever type of berry she's using, she follows the directions for blueberry jam on the pectin box. Finally she labels each jar by the name of the anchorage. And opening one in the middle of winter reminds her of a favourite place.

"I call it my jam diary," she says sweetly.

≈ LIVING OFF THE SEA ≈

We thought it would be easy to live off the sea. So, as an experiment, we left on a ten-day trip without much more than a few cans of corned beef, some bread and potatoes.

We took a crab trap and fishing gear, but in the whole ten days caught just one big starfish and a dogfish that tasted awful even drowned in half a bottle of wine. We ate limpets, but didn't like them, and fistfuls of goose-tongue grass.

On the last day of the trip, we tied up beside a big fishpacker in Hunt's Inlet. We could smell their steaks cooking, the odour wafting down through the galley ventilators. One of the crew brought his dinner out on deck and leaned on the rail to talk. He looked down through the open hatch, at Kristin hunched over the stove with big clouds of steam billowing up. She was stirring a pot full of grass where pale, puffed potatoes surfaced and sank like bloated fish. The crewman didn't say anything, and he didn't stay long, but it was one of the low points of our sailing life.

Over time, we've experimented with other seafoods, but not always with great results.

Sea Cucumbers can be found in the clefts of a rocky shore at low tide, or hauled up on a cod jig from a mud-bottomed bay. Like big, gelatinous slugs, they ooze themselves around the hook, and over your hand. Skinned and gutted, they render only four thin strips of meat that we've found very tough and chewy. Some people, apparently, can cook tasty meals with sea cucumbers, but we leave them—and the animals—very much alone.

Sea Urchins are easy to find on the outer beaches, where they grow to a surprisingly large size. Even the bigger animals contain just a spoonful of roe, so any meal might be tainted a bit by guilt. Kristin sauteed the eggs in butter, but the taste was so overpowering we ate very few. She used the leftovers in a sort of chowder, though, that we both enjoyed very much.

Mussels and Clams, being bivalve molluscs, are susceptible to "red tide" or Paralytic Shellfish Poisoning (PSP). We never touch them in the summer—following the old adage about any month without an "R" in its name—and only rarely in the winter. There is no regular PSP testing done on the north coast, so the Department of Fisheries and Oceans simply closes the entire shoreline to harvesting of bivalve molluscs. The animals may or may not be affected, but it's not worth the risk. Captain Vancouver lost a seaman to PSP, one of the few casualties of his entire voyage. He commemorated the death by calling the spot Poison Cove, and by naming a nearby bay for the dead seaman buried there—John Carter. And the Russian trader Aleksandr Baranov saw more than a hundred Aleuts die of PSP in Peril Strait.

The shellfish itself is not poisonous, but it feeds on toxic organisms that sometimes bloom into huge masses. Boaters often run across the "red tide," thick bands of it like tomato soup floating in the dishwater. But that's a misleading term, for not all the organisms that discolour the water are the gonyaulax that carry PSP. There are even subtle differences between the colours of a red tide.

Near the Dundas Islands we crossed a band of orange that stretched from one horizon to another. The water, when we scooped up a sample, was clotted like half-settled Jello, and contained so many millions of organisms that even the diesel exhaust ran orange. It was noctiluca, not gonyaulax, and quite harmless by itself. But on the island beaches, we kept finding dead fish washed ashore. They'd been suffocated in water suddenly depleted of much of its oxygen.

If a clam consumes great numbers of the poison-bearing gonyaulax, the toxin is contained in its flesh until normal bodily processing sweeps it clean again. There's no home test for PSP, unless you have a cat that likes clams, and there's absolutely no assurance that open-water shellfish are safer than others. The risk of poisoning can be reduced in the cleaning and preparation of the shellfish; there are books that discuss this in detail. But I could never enjoy a summer clam bake. One taste sets me tingling.

Paralytic Shellfish Poisoning is a frightful, horrifying thing. On the radio we heard a man describing his experience with

PSP. Soon after a small meal of fresh clams, he'd felt his lips go numb, and then his fingertips. A paralysis spread through his whole body, bit by bit, until his companions were sure he was dead. All through the ordeal, while they loaded him in the boat and rushed him to a doctor, he'd been fully conscious but unable to communicate by even flickering his eyelashes.

I can't think of that man now without wondering about John Carter. "His death," wrote Vancouver, "was so tranquil that it was some little time before they could be perfectly certain of his dissolution." But I keep wondering: Could he have been buried alive in a lonesome bay half a world from his home?

Rock scallops are sometimes found on the north coast, camouflaged among the anemones on the lowest tides. The most delicious of shellfish, they are—like clams—bivalve molluscs susceptible to PSP. But a clutch of them on the rocks of an exposed shore was almost too much to resist one morning.

We paddled along the exposed cliffs on a zero tide. Kristin had the bread knife ready to pry them loose. She moved aside a curtain of weeds and found one bigger than her hand, all knobby and crusted. She tapped it with the knife.

"You know," she said. "This guy could be fifty years old, even more?"

"Really?" I said.

"They live a long time."

She tapped it again. It had been anchored there when I was born. It had seen the tide rise and fall thirty thousand times or more. And it just didn't seem right to pry it off for a noon-time snack.

"Probably loaded with PSP," said Kristin, and covered it again with its blanket of weeds.

Codfish are easy to catch among the kelp patches of isolated rocks. I use a Buzz Bomb on the fishing line rather than a jig. It brings up pan-size fish instead of the monsters that others seem to catch, but the white meat makes a nice change from salmon once in a while.

Squids come every summer, it seems, into the crowded anchorage of Pruth Bay. They rise to the surface at night, zooming like torpedoes this way and that. With a pair of small, multi-barbed squid jigs, we caught a dozen in a few minutes. The decks were smeared with black ink, and we felt rather heartless leaving the animals in a bucket to die, but it was one of the best meals we ever had.

Squids should be cleaned before cooking. Cut lengthwise up the mantle with a knife or scissors and spread it flat; pull off the head, the tentacles and guts in one motion, then remove the hard, plastic-like membrane. Cut off the head forward of the eyes to keep the squid's eight arms and two tentacles.

After our first attempt at living off the sea, we haven't left the dock again without a well-stocked larder. But we often eat something that's come from the water or the surrounding shore. Usually it's just fish and berries and thick stems of goose grass that, briefly simmered in seawater and doused in butter, make a nice, salty vegetable.

It's not enough to live on, but there's a good feeling in being as self-sufficient as possible. And we sometimes go for weeks without stopping at a grocery store; on the north coast, there are more lighthouses than shopping centres.

Of course the dogs are far better at this than us. Old Arlo, on his one long sailing trip, found half a pound of fresh hamburger washed ashore at Lowe Inlet, a stock of meaty bones in Port Hardy, a big lump of sausage in Prince Rupert.

And with a harvest like that, we might try it ourselves again sometime.

≈ DEALING WITH GARBAGE ≈

On a calm, sunny morning there were half a dozen boats anchored in Kynumpt Harbour. Among them was a large motor yacht from Washington State, swinging in the centre of the small bay at the harbour's edge. There was a family on the boat, an older couple and two daughters. And after breakfast one of the girls dropped a bag of garbage in the dinghy and climbed in over the transom.

She rowed toward shore, but halfway there she stopped the boat and tossed the garbage over the side. It floated there, in its orange bag, as she turned the dinghy and rowed back. She brought the oars in, and pulled out the rowlocks, and then a big Bald Eagle came sweeping down from the trees. Wings thrashing, it grabbed at the bag of garbage and ripped it open without even touching the water.

Someone squealed, and pointed; someone lunged for a camera. The whole family stood at the rail and twittered and cooed as the eagle tore its way through their egg cartons and potato peelings. And they gasped as the bird snatched up the orange bag and carried it streaming back to the trees.

I guess it was quite a spectacle for them, to see their great national bird in action like that. And so close. It must have been like a Walt Disney special, but even better because it was happening in real life. They were still chattering like a nest of squirrels as they hauled up the anchor—carefully squirting at the mud-covered chain with a hose—and broke a trail through the scattering eggshells.

At home they'd show off their photographs. A friend would

push up her spectacles and turn the picture against the light. "What's that he's carrying?" she'd say. And someone would tell her, "Oh, an egg carton I think."

And that's the trouble with garbage. It just comes back to haunt you.

In just about every popular anchorage, you'll find bags of it stuffed among the trees, ripped open by eagles or bears. Go looking for the ruined cabins at Oliver Cove and you'll have to wade through piles of rusted cans and rotting paper. You'll stumble on it at Curlew Bay and Captain Cove, as neatly packaged as something left at a curbside.

There's not the tiniest, loneliest beach on the coast that doesn't have some bit of garbage washed ashore, a collection of plastic among the trees. A friend calls it "a pre-packaged oil spill," but at least oil disappears after a decade or two.

Washington State can levy hefty fines on boaters who throw *anything* over the side, even the soapy water from the galley sink. It's only a matter of time before British Columbia adopts the same laws; and the sooner the better.

Garbage is a problem. It always seems twice as bulky when it's not wrapped around bits of food and quarts of milk or juice. It fills up space and it smells, and it has an awful way of breaking loose.

But most cruising boats are never more than three or four days between places where they can properly dispose of their garbage. Namu has an incinerator; Port Hardy and Bella Bella and Prince Rupert have dumpsters at the dock head.

Kayakers go weeks without stopping at those places, but you'll almost never find garbage in the places where the Little People make their camps. They come and go leaving no more sign of their passing than a keel rut in the sand, a flattened spot in the undergrowth. So why can't boaters who could pick up the whole kayak and lay it on the deck—and not trip over it once—do half as well as them?

We're not perfect. We burn what we can in the ashes of a campfire; we throw away potato peels and onion skins. Sometimes we sink tin cans in deep-water channels. But we bring back bagfuls of bottles and foam and squashed cans, and we don't leave our beaches littered with plastic debris. And if everyone did even that much, a lot of the coast really would look the way it did when Captain Vancouver saw it two hundred years ago.

There's no reason in the world why anyone should pack up the garbage and stash it ashore in plastic bags. It's almost as bad as feeding it to the eagles.

≈ THE FISHIN' STATISTICIAN ≈

I used to be hopeless at fishing, absolutely useless. When I was five years old, I hooked the seat of my pants while casting from a bridge, and I never got much better than that.

In our first three years of sailing, my total catch amounted to one tiny salmon, a skinny codfish and a halibut so small that Kristin made me throw it back. But I never gave up. For days at a time, mile after mile, I dragged an assortment of lures and plugs behind the boat. Even when the hooks got thick with rust, I kept on trying.

"Maybe we should get a book," said Kristin.

I knew what I was doing, I said. I'd worked on a salmon troller.

"Oh," she said. "I don't know what my father would say if he knew I was with someone who couldn't catch fish."

And then she went home on a holiday, and came back with her dad's fishing rod, and a book called *How to Catch Salmon*. It changed everything, using a rod instead of a tangle of line wrapped around a bit of plywood. We had a flasher and a few hoochies, and we mounted a rod-holder in the cockpit, then sat back and waited for the fish to bite. And we waited. And we waited.

We passed the Canoon River late in the summer, when the fish were lining up to get upstream. They leapt and splashed on both sides of the boat. We circled round and round, then I went below to re-read chapters of *How to Catch Salmon*. And when I came back, I could see the flasher skimming along the surface like a water skier.

"That won't work," I said.

"Let's just try it," said Kristin. "Nothing you do works any better."

"Hey," I said. "I worked on a salmon troller." And suddenly, I remembered the secret. I reeled in the gear and cut off the leader between the hoochie and flasher. I measured a new length of line, stretching it along my arm from my outstretched fingers to my nose. I cut it there—exactly there—and put on a new hook. And that night we had our first-ever salmon barbecue. Now we catch salmon almost whenever we want. We slow the boat, put out the gear, and we usually have our fish within the hour. We just do exactly the same thing every time, fishing by statistics:

Gear

On the end of our fishing line is a little spring clip; everything just attaches to there so it can be taken quickly off and stowed complete when not in use. The business end of the gear begins with a steel leader and then a good, hefty weight—four to six ounces of stream-lined lead with swivels at each end. Twenty feet or so of thick monofilament connects to the flasher. Of course every fish is reeled in only as far as the leader, and the rest of the gear is taken in by hand. But it's immensely strong—we're not fishing for the sport of it.

Depth

I put the flasher in the water and let it stream back until it just sinks under water. Then I put my thumb on the reel and, using it as a brake, let off twenty-seven little snatches of line. Sometimes I let off thirty snatches, sometimes twenty-five; it probably doesn't matter at all.

Speed

I set the boat's speed by watching the flasher when it first starts turning. It should make complete circles, but not thrash around like a dog chasing its tail. And once the gear's set, I watch the movements of the fishing rod. The tip should move back and forth at a steady pace, like the masthead of a rolling boat. If it doesn't move at all, we're going too fast; if it shakes and vibrates, we're going too slowly. It should wave slowly and gently; like the queen on a walkabout.

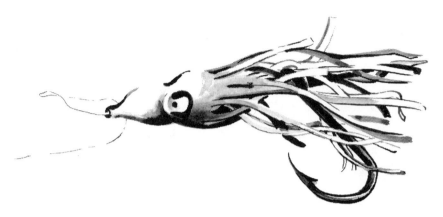

Hoochies

I always use a green one, a small thing about the size and colour of a little Gerkin pickle. After a while I find a lucky one, and keep with it. The best hoochie we ever had caught us scores of fish. We used it for two years, until Kristin snagged it on a crab-trap line in Port Hardy bay. I didn't speak to her for almost twenty-four hours.

Fishing spots

Along the shoreline seems to be best: very close if the bank is steep and rocky. We often fish in the lee current behind long points, or anywhere where the tide rips make long, swirling lines on the surface. Places where seabirds are active seem to be likely spots.

Superstition

We never boast about fishing. It's not hard to jinx a hoochie, and we've gone a week without a salmon barbecue after a careless boast, or a promise to catch something for dinner. I never say "I'm going to catch a fish," but always "I'm going to try fishing for a while." And occasionally, we've had more salmon than we can possibly eat.

≈ COPING WITH BEARS ≈

I was never afraid of bears before I met you," says Kristin. She was camping at Glacier Park the night the grizzlies went crazy. She slept with her mess kit under her pillow, convinced that just banging a spoon on the nested pots would be enough to send a thousand-pound bear running frantically into the night. Kristin never worried about bears at all before she met me.

"Why is that?" she says.

Well, at least I've taught her something.

Most of the people we've met say they don't worry about bears on the B.C. coast. Some even tell stories about picking berries on one side of a bush while a bear is working the other. And they say they feel lucky to see the animals prowling along the beaches. I can only envy people like that. Bears scare me; they always have.

In the interior I was charged by a bear. I credit my escape only to the fact that I was on a motorcycle at the time. Oh, people laughed when I told them about it. But the bear did charge me, thundering up from the bush at the edge of the road, and I did have to swerve out of its way. "Probably a Russian bear," they would say. "He just wanted the motorcycle." I don't tell the story much any more.

But things might have turned out differently one day at Lowe Inlet.

We were walking along the shore at low tide, waiting for the southeaster to die down in the channel. It was nearly sunset, and our little dog followed behind us, zigzagging up and down the beach like a ship beating to windward. And in the mud below a creek, we found the footprints. They were huge.

The dog barked at something, then came running straight to us, the faithful thing. And out in the anchorage, a man hopped into a Zodiac and came roaring across the bay. He stopped the motor fifty yards off, and stood up to shout at us. "Get away from there!" he said.

Kristin humphed. "Why?!" she said.

"There's a grizzly bear behind you," he said, then yanked the starter cord and spun the boat in half its length.

"Oh," said Kristin.

I picked up the dog, and we hurried along the arc of beach to the dinghy we'd left at the falling tide. We pushed it out and tumbled in.

"That was close," I said.

We rowed over to thank the man. ("We must have seemed pretty rude," said Kristin. "Running off like that.") He told us how he'd been watching the grizzly dragging something up the creek bed when we stumbled onto its footprints.

"It was right there not five minutes before you," he said. "When your dog barked, it took off into the bush. I was going to get the gun but—Well, I thought I'd better hurry."

That night we saw the bear, just after dark, plodding along the beach. He came right around the long arc, swaying from side to side, stepping over huge logs and clambering over rocks without the slightest change of pace. He walked right by us and vanished up in the trees where we'd landed with the dinghy.

Perhaps we should have come away from there with a reassurance that bears really do avoid people if they can. But the image of that animal plodding along in the dark, intent and unhurried, was a frightening one. They're big; they can run three times faster than Ben Johnson. And they kill people.

When I confessed my fear to my older brother, I was sure he would laugh. He's gone hiking alone in the Rockies, canoeing in northern Ontario. He had a bear poke its head in his tent. And I thought that, like Kristin, he'd never worried about them.

"They scare me," I said. "I don't know why." And my brother did laugh. "Maybe it's the teeth," he said. "Or the claws."

Just knowing that others feel the same way is reassuring somehow. One popular guidebook says the best way to deal with bears is to remain safely on the boat. But that's going too far even for us. And over time, we've learned to cope with a fear of bears. We just take precautions.

Salmon barbecues are among our favourite things. We usually travel until mid-afternoon, and often end up cooking our salmon over a twilight fire. So we pick islands for our barbecues, little ones. We've sat on some tiny pinnacles of rock, jagged as dragon's teeth, that hardly had enough level space to put down the tea kettle. Sometimes we've felt foolish, but we've often lounged around cold ashes late into the night, and we've never worried about bears over dinner. And, as a bonus, we don't have much fear of setting whole forests on fire.

When we walk in the woods, we make noise. The idea's just to let bears know we're coming; we don't carry ghetto blasters or anything like that. Kristin insists on whistling, though I've told her the sound is distressingly similar to a wounded animal. I just crackle more branches than I have to; call the dog's name a lot. We haven't seen any bears in the woods; and we've never lost the dog.

We avoid river mouths in spawning season, or anywhere else where the ground's beaten down with tracks the size of dinner plates.

We prefer the outer coast to the mainland inlets. It's our natural choice, not made from fear of bears, but grizzlies don't usually wander beyond the mainland.

We don't let it spoil our fun.

I hear on the radio now that a Canadian inventor is working on bear armor. He talks enthusiastically of his massive suit of chainmail and titanium. It weighs as much as he does, and boosts his height from five-foot-eight to seven-foot-two. He describes the onboard computer, the television camera and screen that lets him see, in black and white, any bears lurking in the electronic scenery. It seems he has a few bugs to iron out; the suit can't be worn for more than half an hour at a time, and the wearer, with his air pump, has to be tethered by cables to a tree. But there's hope there, somewhere.

One of the first sailing trips I made with Kristin was up to

Khutzeymateen Inlet, the grizzly capital of Canada and now a marine park. There were two bear biologists working in the valley, and they offered to take us up the river. They armed themselves with shotguns and little cans of bear spray. We thought that was pretty funny, bear spray.

"It doesn't hurt them," said one of the biologists, misinterpreting the looks of worry on our faces. "It sort of bothers them."

There was something odd about the idea of squirting something at a charging bear just thirty feet away and hoping you could bother it. But other people have told me the stuff works amazingly well; like a whiff of garlic to a vampire.

We went up in a Zodiac, through masses of shorebirds that pecked at rotting salmon carcasses. Every now and then, a biologist got out and pulled the boat over a shallow spot. The trees closed in around us, and we landed by a grove of cedars. There was a bit of hair stuck in the bark of one, higher than I could reach. "How did it get up there?" I asked.

"He was standing up," said the biologist.

He told us to be very quiet. We were going to sneak up on the grizzlies in their favourite berry patch. We set off along the bear trail. We passed a mound of scat, still warm and steaming. We stopped at a thick fold of bushes. One of the biologists pried them apart. The other reached for the bear spray.

But there was nothing there.

At the time I was quite relieved. But now I'm sorry there wasn't a whole family of the giant bears browsing through the bushes of the Khutzeymateen valley. For what we saw that day made me think of bears as something very valuable; almost sacred. We saw their trails.

Generations of grizzlies had made craters in the earth. Each one walked in the footsteps of the one before, and the holes were worn deep and smooth, further apart than a man could step. There was a feeling in the air, like a cathedral silence. A waiting.

And it would be an awful thing, if there were no bears out there. We learned something from the biologists: even people who work with bears every day carry some form of protection. So we went looking in the sporting goods store for cans of pepper spray. The salesclerk whisked out a pair of canisters.

Kristin looked at the price. "Sixty dollars!" she said, and put down the cans as though they were Spode china. "I'd rather be eaten by a bear."

"No, you wouldn't," said a man at the fishing goods. He was buying lures and hooks. "Believe me," he said. "You really wouldn't."

But we couldn't afford sixty dollars, and we wandered through forests and meadows as we always had—a bit uneasily—until we met a couple of DFO creek watchers down the coast.

"Boat horns," they said. "In Alaska people are using those little Freon-powered fog horns. And they're having good results."

It was a simple, affordable solution. My brother came up on the ferry and met us in Bella Bella with an extra foghorn. Whenever we went to shore, we slipped one into a packsack pouch, and I had no doubt it would work after I leaned back in the dinghy and accidentally set off that piercing, whooping shriek. I unscrewed the horn, packed it separately, and never worried much after that. And soon, my brother too was carrying a little bear scarer wherever he went.

"It's a good idea," he said. "And I guess if people don't believe it works, they could take one down to Stanley Park and try it out at the zoo."

≈ THE SEA-GOING DOG ≈

There's no reason not to take a pet on a coastal cruise, as long as the animal has some sort of sea sense. If your dog can't walk down the open grill of a gangway without its legs turning to jelly—if you have to manoeuvre your cat through the doorway like an open umbrella—leave it at home. But don't give up hope just because it topples over the side once or twice; good boat dogs are hard to find.

We used to make weekend cruises in company with friends in their twenty-foot sloop. They took four dogs with them, and, though one was so small it was almost a cat, the others were very big. That was an advantage in a way, because our friends could always hear the splash when one of their animals went overboard. Almost every night we'd hear our friend struggling to haul a fifty-pound dog out of the water as it clung to the anchor chain, and then dashing back to the cockpit before it could shake off the cold spray. Sometimes there'd be two or three in the water, one following the next like a stack of marbles.

We've taken two dogs sailing, though not at the same time. The first one was so old that Kristin made a sling for him, so we could hoist Arlo in and out of the dinghy in his suitcase. He'd go ashore in strange towns and people would make jokes about his sea legs as he tottered along the docks. They didn't know he was always like that; Arlo was more than a hundred years old. In rough weather, he just lay on the cabin sole, sliding back and forth with the roll of the boat. But he was a real boat dog, and too good a friend to leave behind.

When he died, we got the Skipper. On her first boat trip, she walked right off the transom and into the water. But now she stands on the deck in the roughest weather, her leeward legs locked straight, her windward ones working like gimbals. She likes to sit at the very eyes of the boat and stare down—hypnotized—at the rush of water round the bow. At anchor she stretches out belly-flat on the lazarette and watches the shoreline endlessly for passing otters.

The Skipper has her own berth, and swaths of fishnet to keep her out of ours. And for the first week or two of each summer's voyage, the dog is a perfect companion. But then she goes crazy, a bit at a time, and turns from Billy Budd to Wolf Larsen. She growls and snaps at both of us. And then Kristin has to scoot into the V-berth each night, sure that the Skipper is going to take a nip at her bottom.

Kristin would just as happily go sailing without the Skipper.

It seems that cats often make better boat pets than dogs. We've met people who sailed halfway around the world with two furry, puffball cats. At anchor the animals would sprawl on the framework of the windvane bracket, hop in and out of the dinghy. They were more at home on the water than most mermaids.

A fishing couple we know takes their cat on the boat all summer. It has a ladder leading up the side of the gillnet drum to its private lair under the dinghy. But Kristin's cat hated boats so much it made every passage sealed in a cardboard box. And other friends had to make two trips to a nearby anchorage when the cat wandered off the first time and refused to come back to the boat. So maybe animals are just like people; some of them like boats, and others don't.

If you do take your pet cruising:

~ DO encourage it to use the same spot on the deck for its natural functions. Skipper happily uses the foredeck, even when the boat's heeled at thirty degrees and plunging along in a heavy chop. A bucket of water sluices it clean.

~ DON'T let a dog bark all night in a crowded anchorage.

~ DO keep a harness on the dog if the sea's anything less than calm. Skipper's safety line is permanently attached to a deck cleat and fitted with a proper snap hook. Once in a while, we have to unwrap her from the mast, but if she ever falls over we only have to reel her in. If there's any sort of wind, an animal's head would be a very hard thing to find in the water.

~ DON'T store cheese in mesh bags. It cost us five dollars worth of fresh cheddar to learn this.

~ DO give the animal its own spot down below. The best thing is to let it pick the place itself, and then fit yourself around it.

~ DON'T let pet food get loose in the cabin. If it ends up in the bilge it turns into a soggy, pump-clogging mess.

~ DO give animals lots of fresh water. They get thirsty in a salty environment.

~ DON'T forget to have the animal vaccinated if you'll be crossing international borders. Customs officials will want proof of rabies vaccination, or they won't let you in.

≈ BY THE BOOK ≈

Required Reading

There are three reference books that every boater travelling on the north coast should keep close at hand.

Sailing Directions – British Columbia Coast (Department of Fisheries and Oceans). Updated regularly, this publication is invaluable and indispensable. Also called the *Pilot*, it describes in great detail every feature of the coast. Extensive front material discusses weather patterns and tidal flow. With a copy of this, and the proper charts, the cruising navigator can go wherever his boat will fit. Volume 1 is the south coast, Volume 2 the north, with the dividing point at Cape Caution. Both volumes are usually available wherever charts are sold. There is also a condensed version specifically for small-craft operators.

Canada Chart No.1: Symbols and Abbreviations (Canadian Hydrographic Service). We call it "the green book," our thirty-four-page guide to the symbols and abbreviations used on Canadian navigation marine charts. If everyone had one, we wouldn't have been asked such embarrasing questions as: "What are these little crosses all over the chart?" (rocks), and "Then why are all these rocks in a straight line?" (the Canada-U.S. border).

Canadian Tide and Current Tables, Volume 6 (Department of Fisheries and Oceans). North of Cape Caution, tides for almost all places on the B.C. coast are referenced to either Bella Bella or Prince Rupert. The only exception is the west coast of the Charlottes, referenced to Tofino. Volume Six of the tide tables covers the entire northern coast and most of Vancouver Island, and includes secondary current stations for the northern narrows.

List of Lights, Buoys and Fog Signals: Pacific Coast (Canadian Coast Guard). This isn't a book that we refer to every day, or even every month. But we've been very glad to have it the few times we needed it. It lists the characteristics of every lighted aid to navigation in British Columbia, a handy tool when you're trying to make sense of a dozen flashing lights on a night passage along the coast.

Recommended Reading

Many books have been written about travels on the Inside Passage. This is not meant to be an exhaustive list, but just a few of the ones we have enjoyed.

North Coast Odyssey by Kenneth Campbell (Sono Nis Press, 1993). This book is subtitled "The Inside Passage from Port Hardy to Prince Rupert." It is in part a history of the B.C. coast, in part a guide to the waterways and landscapes of the real Inside Passage, the route followed by the B.C. Ferries. Designed for a northward voyage, its "Travellers' Guide" is a mile-by-mile description of the Inside Passage as it is and as it was. It should be carried on every boat, as accessible as the flare gun.

Journeys Through the Inside Passage by Joe Upton (Whitecap Books, 1992). Subtitled "Seafaring Adventures along the coast of British Columbia and Alaska," this book also begins in the south and works northward. Each chapter covers a different segment of the Inside Passage, recounting in anecdotes the experiences of mariners over two centuries. We read it like a bedtime story, a few pages a night, then passed it on to a friend who was going down the Inside Passage for the first time. He mailed it back from Vancouver with a message inside: "GREAT BOOK!"

How to Cruise to Alaska by Walt Woodward (Nor'Westing Inc., 1989). The intent of this book is summed up in its subtitle: "Without rocking the boat too much." It is a guide for the small-boat navigator northbound from Olympia to Skagway. It is a cautious look at the popular route along the Inside Passage, designed specifically for those making the trip for the first time.

Charlie's Charts: North to Alaska by Charles E. Wood (Charlie's Charts, 1986). Probably the best of the cruising guides, Charlie's Charts was our Bible on our first trip south. It gives endless help to boaters negotiating the Inside Passage from Victoria to Glacier Bay, detailing every mile of the true Inside Passage and every anchorage the cruiser is likely to need. Unfortunately, the book is hard to find in Canada.

Fundamentals of Kayak Navigation by David Burch (Pacific Search Press, 1987). Though written specifically for kayakers, this book is an excellent lesson in pilotage for anyone travelling in a small boat.

Northwest Passages, Volume II by Bruce Calhoun (Miller Freeman Publications, 1972). The first volume of this collection of cruising stories (not all by Mr. Calhoun) covers the area from Olympia to Desolation Sound. Volume II goes north to the Alaska Panhandle. Though of limited help, the book gives an overall description of the Inside Passage. It is interesting to see how things have changed since these stories were written, more than twenty years ago.

Exploring the Seashore in British Columbia, Washington and Oregon by Gloria Snively (Gordon Soules Book Publishers, 1978). This is an older book, but one of the best guides to intertidal plants and animals of the Pacific coast. Colour photographs and pen-and-ink drawings identify just about everything you're likely to find.

Hotsprings of Western Canada by Jim McDonald (Waterwheel Press of Vancouver, 1991). Though covering a huge area, the book contains a section on hotsprings of the northern coast. Good maps show exactly where the springs are found, and technical chapters explain the workings and history of these hard-to-find spots.

The Voyage of George Vancouver 1791-1795 (Hakluyt Society, London, 1984). Published in four volumes, this work includes the complete manuscript of George Vancouver's *A Voyage of Discovery to the North Pacific Ocean and Round the World 1791-1795*. Only a small portion applies to Vancouver's exploration of northern British Columbia, but it's a fascinating story for anyone with an interest in the history of the coast. Extensive footnotes expand on Vancouver's journal and reference his entries to specific place names.

≈ PARTING SHOTS ≈

On the last page of our first logbook, Kristin started writing down bits of information she'd picked up from other boaters. She called it "Good Advice" and has it memorized. There are only six items on her list:

"When in doubt, get the hell out." A word of wisdom from a former deep-sea sailor, it reminds us that a boat is a lot safer in the open sea than it is among the rocks and reefs of an unknown shore. Heeding this advice, we crossed Queen Charlotte Strait twice in a northwesterly gale rather than find our way into Blunden Harbour for the first time. We ripped the top panel off the staysail, and tore the mainsail when we jibed back. We had buckets of water tossing into the cockpit and the foredeck buried in the waves. But we arrived safely in Beaver Harbour, and crossed the straits for the third time early in the morning in a glassy calm.

"Always remember the tide." Kristin forgot it once, and found her skiff hanging from its painter off the gangway in Sointula. I forgot it and let our boat dry up at Welcome Harbour. We both forgot it in Grenville Channel, and spent hours fighting a flood tide to fetch Lowe Inlet long after dark. But even Captain George Vancouver forgot the tide more than once, and watched tents and watercasks drift away from lonely campsites.

"If the lights clash, you're going to crash." The best of the rhyming mnemonics, this couplet not only eliminates night-time collisions, but whole verses from archaic rulebooks. Kristin insists it should be: "If you clash, you're gonna crash." She's quite

indignant about it: "That's the way my sister-in-law taught me." And that's the way she wrote it in the book.

"If it's not broken, don't fix it." This goes without saying. We're still cleaning oil stains off the cabin sole because I just *had* to check the motor oil once—while the diesel was running. But it's easy to take this bit of advice too far. Kristin heard a funny ticking sound coming from the engine, and begged me to see what it was. I told her a bit of fishing gear was swinging from its hook, tapping on the wall. And it took me an hour to lift the motor cover and find the alternator spitting little lightning sparks. By then the batteries were hot and bulging, and the alternator was ruined.

"Bow line first out of the boat." "The dinghy broke loose," I told Kristin, after I forgot to tie it to the stern cleat. And I dutifully spliced on new rope rather than tell her the truth. "Well, look at that ratty stuff you've been using," she said. "No wonder it broke." But nobody just lets a boat drift away; it's always the boat itself that's somehow at fault. At Safety Cove, my brother and I flipped the dinghy upside down and put a patch on the bottom. I said I'd paddle it to shore like that, and he could follow in his kayak. But I was only halfway there, fighting a headwind, when I heard Donald whistle and shout. "The kayak got away!" he yelled across the anchorage. And—not may people know this—empty kayaks drift at just about the speed a man can paddle an upside-down dinghy. For a couple of days afterward, I kept tripping over cleats that just bulged with rope; Donald's kayak had an extra-long painter. Then he came back from a trip around Schooner Retreat, climbed out of his kayak and into the boat. "Oh, oh," he said. And when I looked up, he was staring at the kayak as it drifted away for the second time. "It's done it again," he said.

"Beware of the lee shore." Perhaps the best advice of all: don't go anywhere you can't get yourself out of.

≈ INDEX ≈

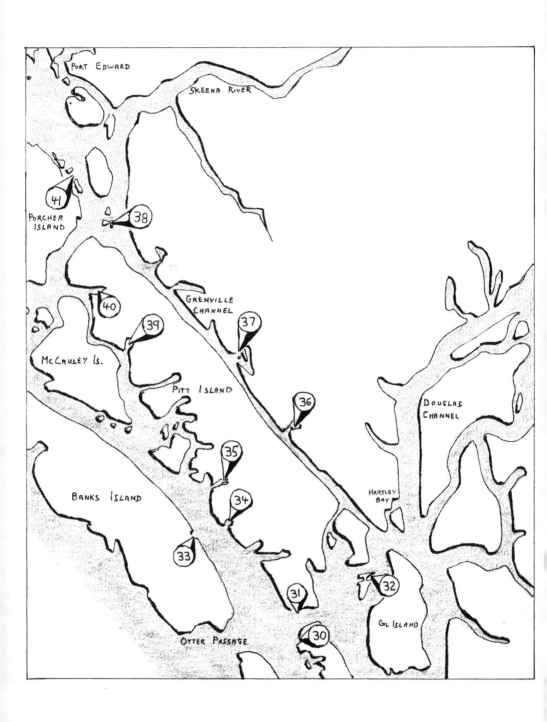